S.W.A.T.
TEAM MANUAL

by Robert P. Cappel

Paladin Press
Boulder, Colorado

S.W.A.T. Team Manual
by Robert P. Cappel

ISBN 0-87364-169-8
Printed in the United States of America

Published by Paladin Press,
a division of Paladin Enterprises, Inc.
Gunbarrel Tech Center
7077 Winchester Circle
Boulder, Colorado 80301, USA
+1.303.443.7250

Direct inquiries and/or orders to the above address.

Visit Our Web site at www.paladin-press.com

INTRODUCTION

The contents of this manual provide guidance and insight into operational procedures, tactics, and theories pertaining to Special Weapons and Tactics (SWAT) Operations. This manual is by no means "all inclusive." However, as one who has researched this subject in depth during the past six years, I will say it is the most definitive and complete manual known to me at this time.

This manual <u>does</u> <u>not</u> prescribe departmental policy in any given situation, rather, it provides information and illustrates procedures that will be required to make a sound decision when employing a SWAT unit.

Robert P. Cappel
Captain Infantry

The mission of the Special Weapons and Tactics (SWAT) Team is to provide ready response to situations beyond the capabilities of normally equipped and trained law enforcement agency personnel. Normally, the operational employment of the SWAT Team will be in response to activities in one or more of three basic (general) areas. The first of these is any situation in which a building or dwelling must be cleared, i.e., barricaded persons, subjects with hostages in a building, snipers in buildings, raids, etc. The second encompasses operations which take place in non-built up areas, i.e., parks, woods, recreational areas. An example of this type operation is an escaped criminal located and contained in a wooded area. The criminal is armed and has taken a defensive position. The third situation will often occur concurrently with with either of the above. This is a hostage situation. In addition to these three primary areas, SWAT can be effectively employed in the security of dignitaries or VIPs, training of non-SWAT personnel, conducting countersniper operations in a Civil Disturbance Environment, and the apprehension (serving warrant and subsequent arrest) of criminals with backgrounds of violent action.

Depending on departmental policy, a SWAT Team may be mobilized for other additional operations. I would encourage this as often as possible. Whether the team is employed or not, is of no importance initially. That the team responds rapidly, with proper equipment, is. Opportunities to employ the team in diversified situations should not be overlooked.

INDIVIDUAL QUALIFICATIONS

The team member of any given SWAT organization must meet specific qualifications.

Mentality: The team member or applicant must be of average,

or above average, intelligence. He must be one who seeks constantly to improve his knowledge, especially in those areas within the realm of his employment as a member of the team. He must be innovative in the approach to his duties and constantly alert.

Physical Ability: The member or applicant must be a mature, stable individual possessing sound judgement and superior reasoning abilities. It must be noted that at any time the team may be inserted into a life or death situation. The decision to take a human life is an awesome one, yet it must be made if necessary, in a fraction of a second. This is a decision that any man on the team (not just the leader), depending on the situation, may one day have to make. In addition to the above, the member or applicant must have a completely positive attitude, regardless of the adverse conditions he is likely to encounter. His esprit de corps, so to speak, must be high. He must adapt to becoming a solid team member, and as such, a vital part of the SWAT concept's strength. THERE CAN BE NO INDIVIDUAL ON A (SWAT) TEAM.

TEAM ORGANIZATION

For the purpose of this section, we will discuss three types of teams. The first is the four-man team, the second is the six-man team, and the third is the eight-man team. These teams will be discussed as singular teams. A department is encouraged to have two or three teams on its squad, which operate together, with the overall Officer in Charge (OIC).

The four-man team: Advantages in this structure are that the unit can be easily controlled by the team leader, and it is large enough to carry a variety of weapons and equipment that may be required. However, if operating independently, with no backup of other teams, a number of disadvantages exist. The mission assigned must be commensurate with the size of the unit. A four-man team alone could not effectively clear a large

department store with numerous floors. The team will not be
able to sustain itself for long periods of time in a firefight.
The loss of one man will severely handicap the team. The team
will have limited flexibility. If perhaps three four-man teams
or more are deployed together, these disadvantages will cease
to exist.

The six-man team: All advantages as with the four-man team
exist here. Disadvantages also apply, but not to the degree of
the single four-man team. If three six-man teams are deployed,
disadvantages will also cease to exist.

Regardless of the team structure, the key to a successful
operation will be found in the decision as to how many teams will
be required, and the level of training and readiness each team
employed has attained.

Notes: NEVER commit a SWAT Team to a situation that is beyond
         its organizational ability and level of training to
         neutralize.

         ALWAYS insure that sufficient teams of well trained
         personnel are committed.

         There can never be "enough" trained teams in any one
         department. The optimum in trained teams would be for
         each member of a department to be trained in SWAT op-
         erations and assigned to a team within the department.
         This solution is highly unlikely. Therefore, to achieve
         results as close to the optimum as possible, as many
         personnel as possible on a department should be trained
         in SWAT operations and assigned to a team in the depart-
         ment. Training sessions for these personnel should be
         scheduled regularly and closely monitored.

Eight-man Team Concept: The team consists of:

   Team Leader: Carries in addition to normal individual equipment a radio; his weapon is an M16 rifle.

   Sniper: Carries in addition to normal individual equipment a radio; his weapon is a scoped bolt action rifle, caliber .223 or more.

(2) Asst Tm Ldr: Weapon is a 12 Gauge Automatic Shotgun; carries normal equipment; carries grenade launching adaptor for shotgun.

(2) Tm Member: Carries 12 Gauge Pump Shotgun (extended magazine encouraged) and normal equipment.

(2) Tm Member: Carries M16 rifle and normal equipment.

Notes: Normal equipment as mentioned above is itemized in this manual.

Personnel armed with the M16 carry a basic load of twelve magazines. Each man will also carry one smoke grenade (military type), one CS grenade, and at least one simulator.

Shotgun personnel will carry a basic load of fifty rounds. Twenty-five of these will be .00 Buck. Five will be Slugs. The remainder will be #4-#9. (Blank shells will be carried by Asst Tm Ldrs for the grenade launcher.)

The eight-man team concept provides a great deal of flexibility within the team itself. The sniper may be detached and the team may operate with two smaller teams of three and four men, respectively. The sniper may not be employed as a sniper (due to poor positions accessible or the situation). In this case the team may operate as two four-man teams or as a complete team of eight. In any case the availability of two assistant team leaders assists the team leader in maintaining control at all times. Another positive factor concerning the eight-man team and the weapons that are carried is that the team can sustain itself for long periods of time, and that the shotgun-automatic rifle concept gives tremendous versatility.

The commitment of two or three eight-man teams will provide formidable force, generally able to cope with any situation.

Table of Assignment:

<u>TEAM LEADER</u>

<u>SNIPER</u>

<u>ASSISTANT TEAM LEADER (A)</u>   <u>ASSISTANT TEAM LEADER (B)</u>

<u>TEAM MEMBER</u>   <u>TEAM MEMBER</u>

<u>TEAM MEMBER</u>   <u>TEAM MEMBER</u>

COMMON SWAT ORGANIZATIONS

Four-Man Team	Six-Man Team	Eight-Man Team
1) Team Leader Rifle Semi or Auto Handgun Radio	1) Team Leader Rifle Semi or Auto Handgun Radio	1) Team Leader Rifle Semi or Auto Handgun Radio

2) Sniper
Scoped Bolt Action
  Rifle
(Shotgun if unable
  to snipe)
Handgun
	2) Sniper
	Scoped Bolt Action
	  Rifle
	(Shotgun if unable
	  to snipe)
	Handgun
		2) Sniper
		Scoped Bolt Action
		  Rifle
		(Shotgun if unable
		  to snipe)
		Handgun

3) Security & Assault
Rifle Semi or Auto
Handgun
	3) Security & Assault
	Asst Tm Ldr (A)
	12 Gauge Auto
	  Shotgun
	Handgun
		3) Security & Assault
		Asst Tm Ldr (A)
		12 Gauge Auto
		  Shotgun
		Handgun

4) Security & Assault 12 Gauge Shotgun Handgun	4) Security & Assault Rifle Semi or Auto Member Tm (A) Handgun	4) Security & Assault Rifle Semi or Auto Member Tm (A) Handgun
	5) Security & Assault 12 Gauge Auto Shotgun Asst Tm Ldr (B) Handgun	5) Security & Assault 12 Gauge Shotgun Member Tm (A) Handgun
	6) Security & Assault Rifle Semi or Auto Member Tm (B) Handgun	6) Security & Assault Asst Tm Ldr (B) 12 Gauge Auto Shotgun Handgun
		7) Security & Assault Rifle Semi or Auto Member Tm (B) Handgun
		8) Security & Assault 12 Gauge Shotgun Member Tm (B) Handgun

For the six and eight man team organizations, if the sniper is not used to snipe, he becomes a member of the security & assault team (B) and is armed with a 12 gauge shotgun. The team leader may choose to use his team as a whole or assign missions to each subteam. (CAUTION: These assigned missions must be within the capability of the subteams to accomplish, i.e., clearing a room, etc.) If the leader does split the team, he accompanies the team that is most likely to make contact.

Basic weapons are listed above with each team position. A complete list of equipment carried by the team and by each member is in this text.

Assigned duties such as scouting can be assigned to any team member, as all must be qualified.

Depending on departmental policy, there will generally be more than one team assigned to the SWAT squad or platoon, i.e., three four-man teams, or four six-man teams, etc.

Suggested list of Team Equipment:

Flashlights & Extra Batteries
Mirrors
Door Jams
Tape
Two Coils 150' Goldline or
   Hemp Rope
Snap Links/Carabiners
Swiss Seat Material
Doughnuts
Binoculars
Gas
Smoke
Simulators
Pole Climbers
16 lb. Sledge
Axe
Hammer
Hacksaw
Pliers
Wire Cutters
Assorted Nails
Screwdriver

Pry Bar
Grappling Hook
Compasses
Flares
Medical Dressings
Morphine
Protective Masks
Flak Vests/Armor Vests
Bolt Cutters
Bullhorn
Camouflage Paint
Short Lengths of Rope
Fire Extinguisher
Ammunition
Weapons
Water Can
Flexicuffs/Handcuffs
Camera 60-Second Polaroid
First Aid Kit
Weapon Cleaning Equipment
Spotting Scopes
12' Folding Ladder

Individual Equipment:

Uniform
Web Equipment/Carrying Equipment
Swiss Seat
D-Rings/Snap Links
Doughnut
Ammo Pouches or Shotgun Cartridge
   Belt
Good Boots
Soft Cap
First Aid Dressing
Mirror
Flashlight

Knife
Hand Gun
Assigned Weapons
Ammunition
1 Smoke
1 CS Grenade
1 Simulator
1 Length of Short Rope
Handcuffs
Gloves (Optional)
Watch
Paper & Pencil

This list is not necessarily all inclusive but is a good guide
of recommended equipment.

WHAT CAN YOU EXPECT?

In normal SWAT team operations, there will be three basic
personalities that will be encountered. These are: The radical
activist, the mentally unbalanced, and the criminal.

The Radical Activist: More often than not, those encountered
that fall into this category will be well trained, highly mot-
ivated, exceptionally well equipped, adept in conducting urban
guerrilla war, well rehearsed and prepared for the encounter.
It must be assumed that this person/persons has determined the
time and place to begin the encounter, and as such is thoroughly
familiar with his position, avenues of approach to his position,
avenues of escape from his position, and the likely courses of
action the Law Enforcement Agency (LEA) Personnel will have to
adopt in their efforts to neutralize him. Through his Intelligence System, he will know your tactics, strengths and weaknesses,
and level of training.

His primary tactics will consist of ambushes, sniping incidents,
bombings or threats of bombings, kidnapping, and assassination.
These operational tactics will serve to cause conditions of fear
in the general populace. The logic being, if the police are
seemingly such easy targets, what chance is there for the
average citizen? In numerous publications on the market at
present, in newspapers, and on news reports, statements have
been, and are being, made that the police are primary targets,
"and the streets will run red with pig blood." Even though the
threat presented by this personality is formidable, there are
weaknesses that may be exploited by LEA personnel. For the
LEA that is familiar with the tactics that the radical will
adopt, determinations of the radical course of action can be
made. Once this is accomplished, countermeasures may be planned
and effected. The radical may have a vast amount of equipment

on hand at the time of the encounter, however, he will function
only as long as these means exist. His physical needs must
also be met. If he can be isolated, he will eventually be forced
to surrender or conduct some type of tactical maneuver, other
than what he had planned. Once a situation with this type of
person/persons is encountered, all efforts should be directed
at containing and isolating it. Allowed to move freely before
counterforces have been deployed will almost always result in
the successful escape of the radical. Initially, this force
will have the upper hand on LEA personnel. As the situation
develops, the balance of power will shift to the side of the
police. The team or teams of SWAT personnel that conducts an
assault on a position prepared and manned by a radical group
must be prepared to strike violently with the greatest amount
of professionalism and skill. A final point relevant to the
radical activist is that, whenever possible, they will try to
place LEA personnel in a "bad light." This is often accomplished by intimidating LEA personnel to over-react to a
situation, i.e., headlines read, "Forty Police Storm Vacant
Headquarters of Underground Weathermen, Cleaning Woman Shot
to Death." This incident never happened but certainly could.
LEA personnel must be aware of the exact situation they face
and use the forces available judiciously.

NOTE: See Ambush and Counterambush text in this manual;
also, Sniper/Counter-Sniper.

The Criminal: More often than not, the criminal will have
been caught in the act of committing a crime and taken refuge
on the spur of the moment. He will normally have a very limited
supply of equipment (weapons and ammunition) with which to fight.
It is unlikely that he will have planned a defense. He will
more than likely be unfamiliar with his surroundings. A key
point is that he will not have picked the time and place to

conduct defensive operations, and his position will be hastily chosen at best. The criminal, of the three personalities discussed in this text, will be more apt to listen to reason than the other two. Initially, officers arriving on the scene should attempt to contain and isolate this man. Do not allow him to move to a better position. He will continue to fight until his ammunition is depleted, his physical needs are no longer met, he can be talked into surrender, or he is dispatched by force. Following a criminal to his residence to make the arrest or apprehension may be somewhat different. At his home he may have a tremendous stockpile of ammunition and arms. This situation would be somewhat similar to confronting a radical activist.

The Mentally Unbalanced: Of the three types of personalities to be encountered, the mentally unbalanced is the most dangerous. His actions are totally unpredictable. He may or may not have a definite plan of action. He may or may not be well equipped. This man's actions cannot be anticipated. He is difficult to reason with. A situation involving the mentally unbalanced personality must be handled with extreme caution, especially if hostages are involved.

NOTE: To assist the LEA officer in achieving a better understanding of the radical activist, the following pages illustrate common guerrilla principles of war, as well as listing counter-guerrilla principles of offensive and defensive operations.

COMMON GUERRILLA WARFARE PRINCIPLES

"The guerrilla must be compared to the tiger and the regular forces to the elephant. If the tiger confronts the elephant head-on, the elephant will grasp the tiger with his trunk and dash him to the ground, and trample him to death. However, should the tiger hide in the trees and wait until the elephant passes beneath, he may lunge to the back of the elephant out of reach of the trunk and tear huge pieces of flesh away. Continuing this practice the elephant will slowly bleed to death."

> Mao Tse-tung

Strike where least expected.

Make the enemy think you are strong when you are weak.

Make the enemy think you are weak when you are strong.

Attack only when victory is assured.

Strike in many areas at one time to make the enemy deploy his forces, then make your main attack at an area he has abandoned.

When he attacks, you withdraw.

When he halts or defends, you harass.

When he withdraws, you pursue of attack.

Use bait or lures to ambush the enemy.

Always fight on your ground.

Have escape routes and actions planned.

If you are forced to withdraw, hide your weapons and take up the role of a civilian; once the enemy has passed you, take up your weapon and strike his rear.

If possible, strike the command group. "The most venomous serpent is but a twisting piece of rope when the head has been severed."

> Sun Tzj, 500 B.C.

Use obstacles and booby traps.

Use children and women to scout, create unfavorable public opinion, and carry supplies.

Destroy or jam the enemy lines of communication.

Create public fear by assassinating key public officials/ dignitaries.

Create distrust by exposing any government or LEA scandal.

Before an ambush, rehearse 100 times, include all possible reactions in your training.

Strike with massive firepower.

COUNTERGUERRILLA PRINCIPLES

Principles of Offensive Operations

Gain & Maintain Contact.	Make contact with the enemy. This involves the SWAT team locating and fixing the subject in position. Once this is accomplished, every effort is made to maintain contact.
Develop the Situation.	Comparatively, this is like two boxers feeling each other out. During this time you set the stage for the resolution of the situation.
Exploit Known Enemy Weaknesses.	Again as boxers, one notices the other has lowered his guard and throws the punch. Perhaps you notice the subject has not taken precautions to cover a certain door or window in a building and you are able to enter, or his flank is not protected and you apply pressure there.
Seize & Control Key Terrain.	Any piece of terrain that offers a marked advantage to either side if they can control it is considered as Key Terrain. This could be the roof of a building, a hill, or a stairwell.
Neutralize the Enemy Capability to React.	For instance, a criminal has a getaway car parked near his position. By shooting out his tires you neutralize his capability to use it or react. By sealing the subject off in one room, you deny him freedom of movement and again neutralize much of his capability to react.
Advance by Battle Drill Techniques.	An operational tactic where men move under fire with as much safety as possible. This is explained in detail later in the text.
Maintain the Momentum of the Attack.	Once the attack has begun it must not stop. Maximum pressure is put on the subject.

Provide for Security & Integrity of Forces.	This means that physical security is always used. It also means that teams must operate as whole teams. Two men from one team and three from another would not be as effective as having five men from one team.
Concentrate Superior Combat Power at the Decisive Place & Time.	As the action progresses, it will often become apparent that the enemy is nearly beaten or that more power is required. At this time the leader must be prepared to commit those forces and/or equipment required to assure the favorable outcome of the situation in the right manner at the right time.

Principles of Defensive Operations

Maintain Defense in Depth.	In the event that the SWAT team is assigned the mission of conducting a defensive type operation--protection of federal property of a dignitary, or participating in the cordon of an area--the defense should be more than one line of men. Defense in depth calls for "lines" of defense, with positions from the forward edge of the defense back, in sufficient numbers to contain the situation or provide adequate protection. If one line of defense was all that was provided and that line was infiltrated, the defense would be useless. With a defense in depth, the front line may be infiltrated, but the remaining positions to the rear will stop the infiltration before it reaches its target.
Utilize Good Observation & Fields of Fire.	Positions used in the defense must provide the defender with clear fields of vision and fire.
Utilize Key Terrain	Utilize the terrain that will give you an advantage over your subject.

| Employ Obstacles. | Obstacles can be used to slow movement or restrict it totally. If your team was conducting a building search, and you had cleared a room and were preparing to move on to another one, you could lock the door of the room you had cleared. This would present an obstacle to any party who would try to enter that room behind you. In a cordon operation, a roadblock is an obstacle. |
| Maintain a Reserve. | A reserve force should always be planned for and provided. In the event that any given situation arose that could not be controlled by committed forces, the reserve force could be called upon for assistance. |

AMBUSH AND COUNTERAMBUSH

Ambush is defined as a surprise attack by fire against a moving, halted, or temporarily halted opponent, with the mission of harassment, inflicting casualties, or full destruction. Types of ambushes: For the purpose of this text, ambushes will be divided into two types; the Near Ambush and the Far Ambush.

Near Ambush: The near ambush will be initiated at ranges of from zero to fifty yards. The ambushers will attack from well concealed positions with surprise and overwhelming firepower. The kill zone (that area to the front of the ambush position covered by fire wherein an opponent would be killed by fire immediately) is normally zero to fifty yards to the front of the ambush position. Teams caught in a near ambush have but one course of action to adopt. That is to conduct an immediate assault directly into the ambush position. (This is for those in the kill zone.) Those not in the kill zone must conduct a flanking operation and subsequent attack of the position. It will be more dangerous for the unit in the kill zone to assume a prone position and return fire than to assault. The reason is that

most ambush positions will facilitate total destruction of
anything in the kill zone, regardless of whether it is standing,
sitting, or in a prone position. Most kill zones will have
been "prepared," i.e., voided of any cover. By taking the immediate action prescribed, you will force the ambushers to fight in
two or possibly three different directions, when the ambush was
planned for fighting only in one direction. See FIGURE ONE:
Immediate Action to a Near Ambush.

Far Ambush: The far ambush will be initiated at ranges from
fifty yards to the maximum range of the weapons used. When
caught in an ambush of this type, example 150 yards, the team
will attempt to find cover and return fire. Those members not
in the kill zone will attempt to maneuver against the ambush
position. Battle Drill (as discussed later in this manual)
may be used by the unit caught in the kill zone, to attack the
position, if that is the leader's decided course of action.
The unit in the kill zone may break contact, move out of the kill
zone, and deploy to attack in a different direction, or take
cover and provide a base of fire for those who will maneuver
against the ambushers. The kill zone in a far ambush will be
larger than that of a near ambush. The concentration of fire
will be somewhat less, as will the degree of accuracy at the
greater ranges. An excellent aid in assisting a "pinned down"
unit out of a far ambush kill zone is smoke. If it is decided
to pull back, smoke should be thrown between those ambushed and the
ambush position. This will help obscure the movement of those
caught in the kill zone as they pull back. See FIGURE TWO:
Immediate Action to a Far Ambush.

Precautionary measures that may be taken to counter the effect
of an ambush are to maintain good dispersion any time your unit
is on the move. Security to the front, flanks, and rear must
be maintained. This can be accomplished by having selected

personnel walk forward of, to the sides of, and to the rear of the main body. These personnel must be out far enough so that if they spring an ambush they will be the only ones in the kill zone. They must be close enough so that the remainder of the team can cover them with fire support. Taking advantage of all cover and concealment will negate an ambush's effectiveness. Taking listening halts is also beneficial. Each man must be alert and prepared to follow the orders of his leader immediately. Weapons must be ready ALWAYS. A well trained unit may be able to identify an ambush periodically before it is sprung. In the field unexplained cut vegetation is an indication. Vegetation is cut to clear the kill zone, and for camouflage. A lack of normal animal movement and noises can be a good indicator. A "too easy" to follow trail should alert the unit to the possibility of an ambush. In the city an ambush may be discovered or at least suspected when a call is answered and on arrival you find "no" children playing where they should be, adults of a given area avoiding the area (this should also alert one to the possibility of boobytraps in the area), traffic flow in an area stopped or slowed, roads blocked, calls to vacant addresses or non-existing addresses, or gunfire in an area.

NOTE: All members must thoroughly understand and be competent in immediate action drills. Counterambush actions should be practiced continuously. In practice, situations must be made as realistic as possible.

FIGURE ONE: Immediate Action to a Near Ambush

Teams are moving, when they are
ambushed from the left flank.
The center team (caught in the
kill zone) immediately assaults
into the ambush position. The
front and rear teams conduct a
flanking maneuver and also assault
the position.

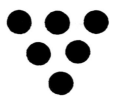

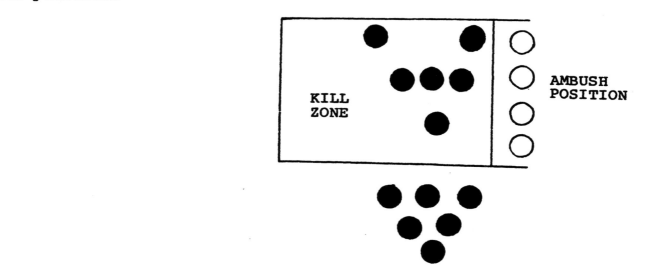

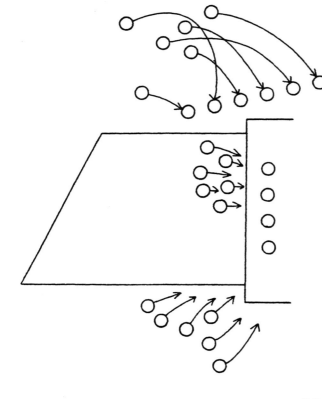

Teams conducting the
assault and proper
flanking maneuvers.

FIGURE TWO: Immediate Action to a Far Ambush

Element in kill zone seeks cover and returns fire. The two elements not in the kill zone can maneuver against the ambush position on the flanks if the leader decides that is the proper course of action. (The unit in the kill zone could act as a base of fire for that type of operation.) All teams could pull back and redeploy as a group to attack the ambush position. (Smoke helps in withdrawal.)

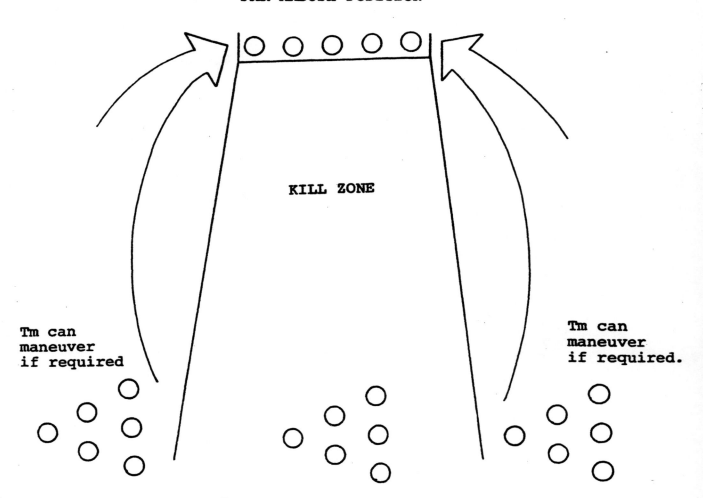

FAR AMBUSH POSITION

KILL ZONE

Tm can
maneuver
if required

Tm can
maneuver
if required.

Tm in kill zone
seeks cover and
immediately returns
fire.

SNIPER/COUNTERSNIPER

Police surveys from 1972-73 indicated that in fifty percent of all ambushes against LEA personnel, snipers fired the first shots, initiating the ambush. The average range for these incidents was eighty yards. An average of two shots were fired by the sniper. Most snipers will fall into the Activist or Mentally Unbalanced personality category.

Always expect that the sniper has provided himself with a position that gives him clear fields of fire and observation. Suspect that the sniper has taken advantage of the use of camouflage, which will make him difficult to distinguish. Try to determine the direction to the sniper by his muzzle crack, or flash at night. Knowing that the sniper is in an advantageous position should rapidly motivate an officer to seek cover. If the cover that an officer finds on the first shot is not sufficient, he should move to a better position rapidly. It takes the average marksman four to five seconds to draw a bead on a moving target. This means that while moving from cover to cover you must not expose yourself any longer than three seconds. All movement of this type should be as rapid as possible. Once your team is in covered positions, the leader makes an estimate of the situation and determines what action will be taken.

FIRST: You must pinpoint the sniper's location. This is done from a covered position using binoculars, or the scope of the team sniper's weapon. After this is accomplished, the situation may be resolved in any of the following ways, depending on the situation.

SNIPER AGAINST SNIPER: Upon locating the sniper's position, the SWAT team sniper engages him with carefully directed fire. The advantages of this type action are; a minimum number of team members will be exposed, the team leader will have excellent control, and firing is very discriminate, leaving little chance of innocent persons in the area being harmed. Disadvantages are that the team sniper may not have a good position to fire from, a miss can cause the subject sniper to flee, more than one subject sniper cannot be engaged, and this method takes much time.

SWAT TEAM AGAINST SNIPER: Using this tactic, the entire team (or teams) moves offensively against the sniper's position. (Movement Techniques are discussed later in text.) The SWAT team sniper (or snipers) supports by fire from a fixed position during the attack. The advantages to this action are; there is more firepower directed at the sniper position, accurate fire from the team sniper (or snipers) will help to keep the subject sniper down and somewhat reduce his fire, more than one sniper can be engaged, the situation is resolved faster, and the psychological advantage is with the attackers. The disadvantages are, more men are exposed and there is the possibility of a control problem over the team (this is dependent of the level of training the team has achieved).

BLOCKING FORCE TECHNIQUE: In this type of operation, additional SWAT teams and snipers are placed along likely avenues of withdrawal of the subject sniper. Once positioned, the attack team begins an assault on the sniper's position. If the sniper withdraws he will more than likely move into the kill zone of the previously placed teams. If he stays in position he will be overrun. The advantages are basically the same as those present when one team or teams attack. Additionally, these teams that have been placed prior to the assault can serve as reinforcements should the main attack be stalled. They may also attack, forcing the sniper to fight in two directions. Disadvantages are the same as with one team/teams attacking. A more complex control problem can arise with additional teams and snipers employed.

NOTE: In all of these operational courses of action, cover and concealment, sound movement principles, and fire support are utilized. The use of smoke to conceal movement or gas to reduce the effectiveness of the subject sniper should be contemplated. These techniques apply to any sniper situation, whether it occurs inside a building or outdoors.

When moving a team into a known sniper situation, take maximum advantage of cover and concealment. Maintain maximum dispersion within the team. Observe at all times. Keep weapons at the ready and be prepared to enact immediate action drills on command.

POSITIONING OF THE TEAM SNIPER: As each situation that is encountered will be different in varying degrees, it is technically impractical to prescribe absolute methods of how a team sniper should be employed. Rather, there are guidelines that if followed and adapted to the situation will prove to be highly effective.

1) Employ your sniper where he has clear fields of fire and observation.
2) Insure that the position he utilizes provides him with Cover and Concealment.
3) Remember he is the best shot on your team. He can be employed at a relatively far distance from the incident that requires his talent. (This in many instances will reduce the possibility of the sniper becoming a casualty.)
4) The location chosen should enable the sniper to provide continuous close fire support for an assaulting element.
5) The sniper must be in communication with the team leader of the assaulting team/teams.
6) He must be thoroughly briefed as to the ground tactical plan and to the scope of his employment.

7) If possible the sniper's position should be on a ninety-
   degree angle to the route of approach of the assaulting
   team. This enables him to provide fire support for a greater
   length of time. There will be times that the sniper will
   be required to support in the direction of the route of
   approach. Close coordination will be required here. See
   examples following:

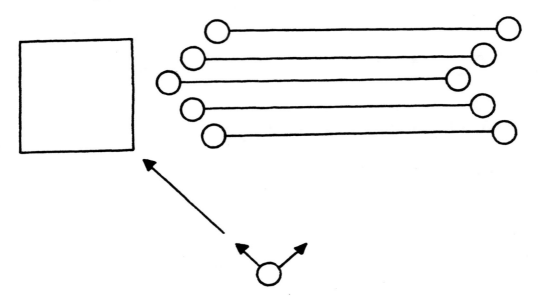

Supporting from a position ninety degrees in relation to the
direction of attack. In this example the sniper can cover the
attacking team from the time they begin the attack until they
reach the objective.

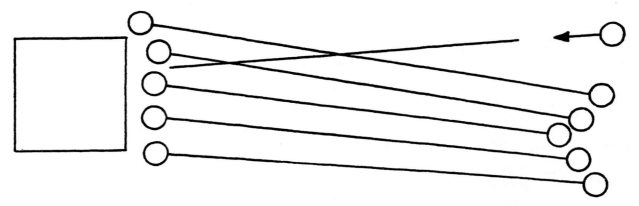

Supporting along the direction of attack. (If the sniper is in a
position that affords height, this type of support will also be
effective.) If no high ground exists, the assaulting team will mask
(block) the sniper's fire eventually and he will be forced to stop
firing.

The following diagrams illustrate proper and improper sniper positioning in different settings.

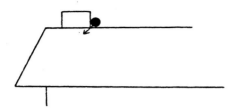

Roof Top (Correct)

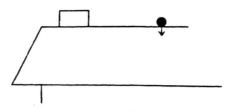

Roof Top (Incorrect)

Vegetation (Correct)

Vegetation (Incorrect)

Corner (Correct)

Corner (Incorrect)

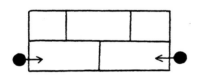

Wall (Correct)

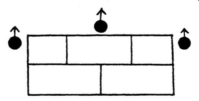

Wall (Incorrect)

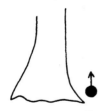

Tree Trunk (Correct)

Tree Trunk (Incorrect)

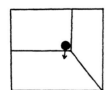

Window (Correct)

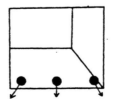

Window (Incorrect)

To assist the SWAT team leader in maintaining control and
providing a ready posture from which to initiate immediate
action drills (discussed later in text), _formations_ are used.

For the purpose of our text we have defined four basic formations. The figures that illustrate these formations in the
following pages indicate a type team of six men. These formations are applicable to any team structure or organization.

Once the basic formations as illustrated are learned and become
reflex actions of the team, variations of each should be practiced. Practicing movement in formations must be accomplished
over varying terrain, from open ground to movement inside a
building. After the minimum amount of time is spent showing each
man his place in any particular formation, training "as if"
in the real situation must become the norm.

As you read through the following pages you will see that each
formation has inherent advantages and disadvantages. More importantly, you should realize that certain formations are used
to accomplish specific missions. They are used according to the
situation.

NOTES ON TRAINING: Initially, it will seem that formation training
is repetitious, boring, and not all that important. Upon closer
examination, you will find that it is one of the most essential
parts of training. More than fifty percent of your time in an
operation will be spent in movement. (Reconnaissance, movement
to objective area, possible assault, consolidation, withdrawal,
redeployment.) It behooves all to know the right way of going
about it. Personnel must always train carrying their weapons
(at the ready). Maximum use of cover and concealment must be
enforced. Observation by all personnel must be stressed until
it becomes a reflex. Practice makes perfect.

FORMATIONS

FILE:

Follow the Leader
Fast Moving
Poor Security Front
Poor Fire to Front
Good Fire to Flank
Easy to Control

TEAMS IN COLUMN:

Fair Control
Good Security
   Front, Flanks
     & Rear
Fast Moving
All Around
   Firepower

TEAM A

TEAM B

WEDGE:

Good Firepower Front
   Flanks & Rear
Fast Moving
Good Control
Good Security
Used When Contact
   is Expected

LINE:

Maximum Firepower to Front
Poor Flank Security
Difficult to Control
Used to Assault or Conduct
   Sweeps/Searches

Leaders ⊕ stay where they can best control the majority of
their personnel.

METHODS OF MOVEMENT

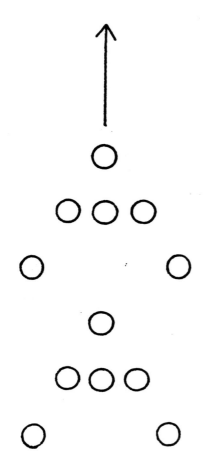

TRAVELING:

Traveling formation is used when contact is not likely. It offers speed and a considerable amount of control.

Notice that there are two wedges. Each team is one wedge, one team behind the other. Members of each wedge maintain appropriate distance depending on the terrain.

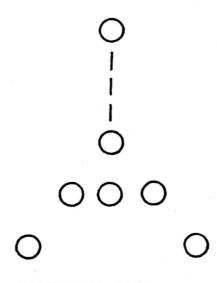

TRAVELING OVERWATCH

Here the lead fire team advances ahead of the rear fire team from fifty yards to the maximum distance from which the rear team can support by fire. The distance between teams will be dependent on the terrain, i.e., in open fields the distance would be great and in heavily vegetated areas the distance would be reduced.

Used when contact is likely.

This puts the minimum number of personnel forward and leaves a free uncommitted team for maneuver.

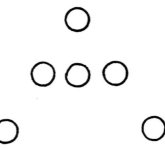

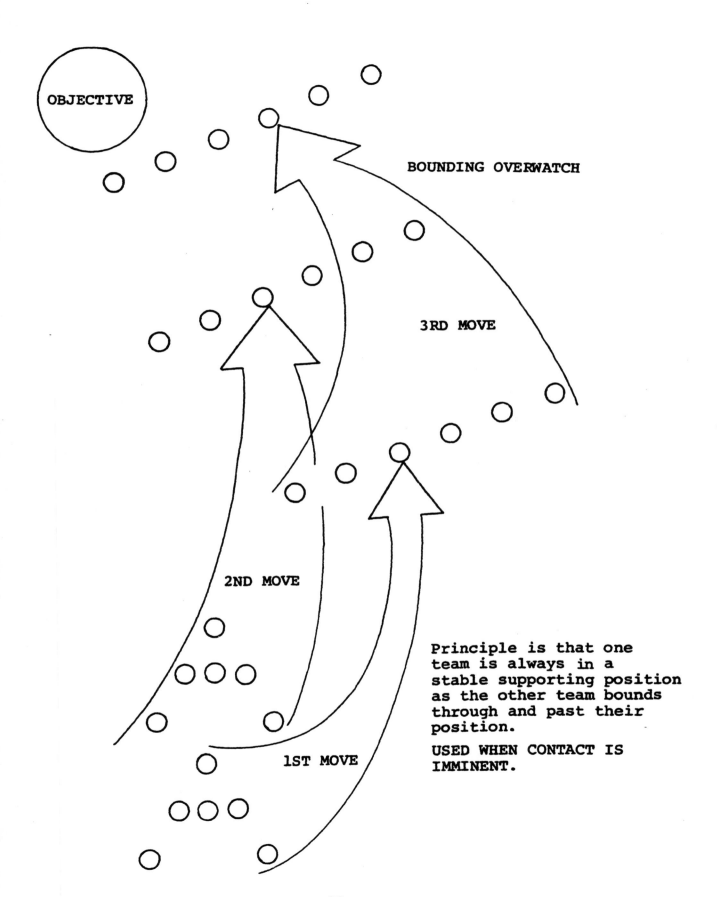

OBJECTIVE

BOUNDING OVERWATCH

3RD MOVE

2ND MOVE

1ST MOVE

Principle is that one
team is always in a
stable supporting position
as the other team bounds
through and past their
position.

USED WHEN CONTACT IS
IMMINENT.

The next portion of the text is dedicated to the conduct of
Battle Drill (Immediate Action Drill). Battle Drill takes over
from the point where you receive fire and begin to maneuver
against it.

The following examples illustrate the two methods of conducting
Battle Drill. These are: Fire and Movement, and Fire and Maneuver.
Any time a team is committed to neutralize a situation and they
must move into the objective area by force, one of the two methods
prescribed or a variation thereof will always be used.

The importance of immediate reaction to a situation (properly
applied) cannot be over-emphasized.

Battle Drill training is without a doubt the one class that I
would continue to train my team in if only one period of
instruction was offered in SWAT training.

TRAINING NOTES: Once the basics have been learned, discard
canned exercises. Employ other team members as barricaded persons
or ambushers at unexpected times and places in training operations.
Initial operations by the SWAT members in reaction to these events
will be for the most part disorganized and poorly handled.
As time progresses, so will the team. The real situation will
not be a canned exercise, therefore training should not be.
Give your ambushers a general area or a number of buildings to
set up in and then ferret them out. (Completely unrehearsed.)
Again, practice makes perfect.

BATTLE DRILL--1

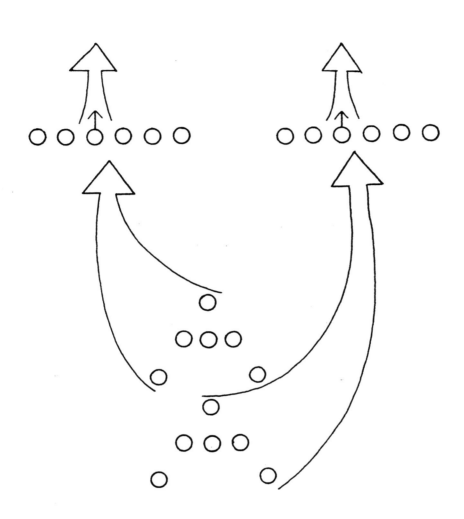

You are in a traveling formation and receive fire from the front.
The squad leader will have you move on line. He will tell one
team to go right and one team to go left. After you are on line
the squad leader will direct your team leader to move by individ-
uals. At this time the team leader will move forward rushing,
no more than three seconds up. This establishes the distance
the rest of the team will move as he calls them and the amount
of time that they may be relatively safe to stay up.

Once he's in position the team leader begins calling his team
forward by previously assigned numbers or by names.

(First move is always made by the team leader.)

BATTLE DRILL--2

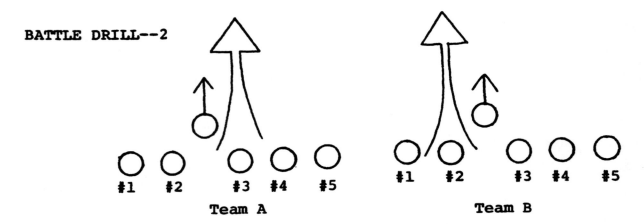

Team leader of Team A calls his #3 man forward. Team leader
of Team B calls his #1 man forward. No set order is established. Avoid setting a pattern of numbers. Each man as called
must move forward relatively straight. Those not moving must
be supporting by fire or if not necessary, prepared to support
by fire.

BATTLE DRILL--3

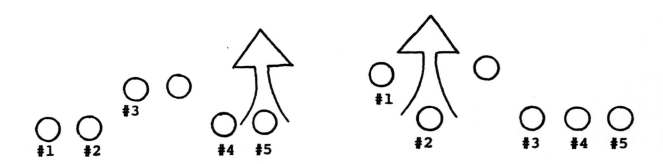

Both team leaders continue calling men forward until the entire
team and squad are on line again. If the firing is still heavy
(coming at you) you may wish to continue to move like this.
If it is not, you may wish to close with the objective faster.
You may do this by moving more than one man at a time. Each
team leader now calls for more than one man to move.

Leader of Team A has moved #2, #3, and #5 man forward. Leader of Team B has moved #2 and #4 man forward. On the command of each team leader the remainder of the teams would move forward and on line. If there is less fire coming at you now, you may wish to move even faster. The squad leader takes command and yells, "A team lay down a base of fire, B team move out." Immediately all of Team B moves forward while Team A covers. (Complete first entire move of teams by moving one at a time.)

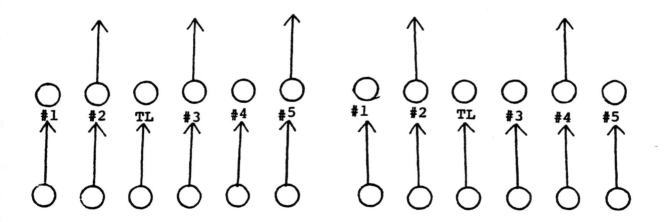

BATTLE DRILL--5

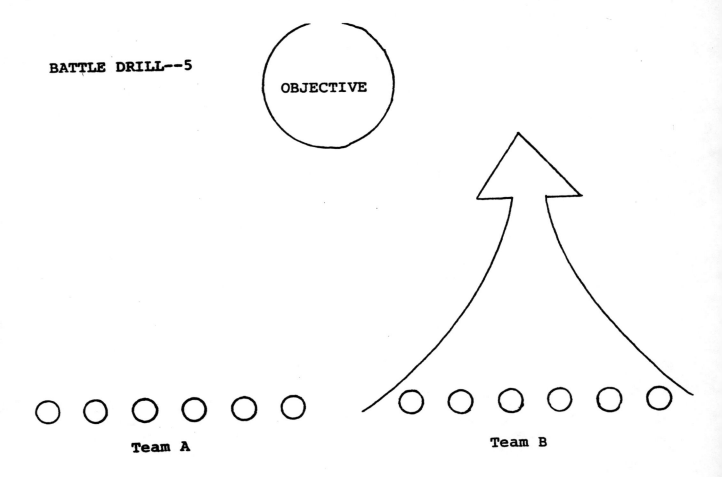

Team B moves while Team A covers.

BATTLE DRILL--6

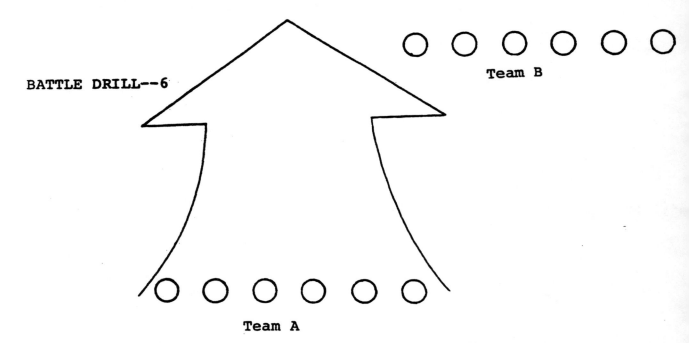

Once Team B is in position the squad leader commands Team B to lay down a base of fire and Team A to move out.

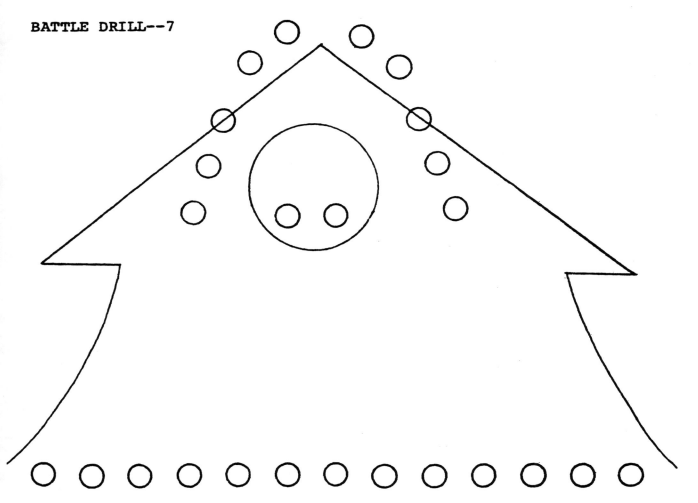

To make the assault the squad leader gets his entire squad as close to the objective as possible. He commands, "Prepare to assault," and all personnel begin to direct a maximum volume of fire at the objective. Simulators and gas may be thrown. He then commands, "Assault," and all personnel move on line in a crouch, firing if necessary as they move to and through the objective. One or two men should be designated to check enemy dead, wounded, or surrendered. If at any time during this operation you should begin receiving heavy fire, you may revert to individual movement, which is slow but effective. After you have gone through the objective, you form a half circle or full circle with the salient angle toward the direction of attack. This is called consolidation. Now be ready to withstand a possible counterattack. You are vulnerable... Redistribute ammo if required, treat your wounded, and prepare to continue on if required.

CLOCK METHOD OF CONSOLIDATION: Break your objective area up so it corresponds to the face of a clock. One team might cover 10-2, another 2-6, and another 6-10. 12 o'clock is always the direction of travel.

TERRAIN METHOD OF CONSOLIDATION: Tie teams in on natural features, i.e., from this bush to that tree, etc.

PRINCIPLE OF FIRE & MANEUVER

OBJECTIVE

Rear element with leader maneuvers
along a covered or concealed route
to the objective. The team then
moves on line and conducts assault
as required. Set team may move
forward to provide closer fire
support. Fires are shifted from
support element when maneuver
element begins the assault. Some
form of communication or visual
signal is absolutely necessary in
this operation. Support element
must be able to cover the entire route
of the maneuver element.

UPON RECEIVING FIRE:
Lead unit fires in
support of rear unit
from an on line
formation.

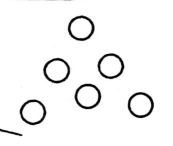

PLANNING THE OPERATION

The successful completion of any operation depends on prior planning, individual and unit training level, and the proper use of individual and team equipment.

The most critical of these criteria is prior planning. Without proper planning prior to commitment in an operation, the team suffers a distinct disadvantage. Numerous methods for planning are used by different teams. The one best method that I would recommend as a format for all planning is the use of the Military Operations Order.

The next three pages encompass the use of this format, as well as illustrating where it is developed in the structure of the Troop Leading Procedure. (The Troop Leading Procedure is a schedule of actions to take upon receiving an assignment or mission.) The overall Troop Leading Procedure and a definitive explanation of the Operations Order follows.

The use of the Operations Order should be a part of each train-ing session, until all personnel on the team are familiar with its structure, and more importantly, its preparation.

TROOP LEADING PROCEDURE

BEGIN PLANNING

Analyze your mission. Determine what you have to do.

Collect all information available from Higher Adjacent and Lower Headquarters.

Analyze Terrain or Objective Area.

Develop possible courses of action.

Determine special aspects, i.e., restrictions, etc.

PRELIMINARY ACTIONS

Issue a warning order to your team.	This tells them only what the mission is, what equipment to prepare, and gives a general time breakdown. Tell when the Operations Order will be issued.
Make a leader's recon of the area.	At a minimum use a map, blueprints, and most favored, recon the area. Observe the courses of action you thought of.

CONTINUE PLANNING

Analyze the courses of action you originally chose and any new ones you determined from you reconnaissance.

COMPLETE PLAN

Coordinate plan.

Complete writing the order.

ISSUE THE ORDER

Insure understanding.

SUPERVISE

Prepare to execute.

Keep Higher and Lower Adjacent Headquarters informed.

OPERATIONS ORDER

1) **SITUATION:**
Enemy Forces: How many, where, what type of equipment/weapons, status, probable courses of action.

Friendly Forces: All forces that are capable of supporting or will support will be mentioned here, i.e., District 1 will cover the Gane St. alley and will back us upon entering the house. Basically, where these units are in relation to yourself on the ground. Include units higher, adjacent, and lower.

Attachments & Detachments: Here you will mention any special purpose equipment or personnel other than what your teams originally carry that you will get, i.e., Canine Team will be attached, Long Range Sniper Team, etc.

2) **MISSION:**
Here you state in plain simple words exactly what your task is going to be. Answer Who, What, When, Where, Why.

Our team assaults at 0900 tomorrow the
WHO   WHAT   WHEN

Sears Bargain Barn to apprehend or neutralize
WHERE   WHY

those personnel who are holding it.

3) **EXECUTION:**
Here you give a brief restatement of the mission and a general picture as to how you are going to do it.

Sub-unit Missions: Here you will give each man or team specific tasks as to what they will do from the time they leave the assembly area until the operation has ended, i.e., Jones, you will be first in the order of movement, I want you to be the cover man on any stairs we encounter. Smith, you will be second, insure you cover Smith on the stairs, also you will be a member of the room clearing team, etc., until all men or teams know exactly how they fit in the overall picture.

Coordinating Instructions: These are instructions that apply to everyone and are essential to the mission, i.e., District 1 police will secure all entrances behind us. There are civilians

in the building who have not been evacuated. Police will attempt a diversion-
ary action to attract the dissidents'
attention commencing at 0855 to insure we
can achieve a successful entrance, etc.

4) SERVICE SUPPORT:
Here you will plan for and obtain all
equipment you will require. You will tell
your personnel how much of and what to
draw, and where to draw it, i.e., Smith
draw four gas grenades from the Scout Car
and 50 rds of #4 shot. Each man draw a
protective mask and flak vest, etc.

5) COMMAND & SIGNAL:
Establish a chain of command all the way
down to the last man. Tell all personnel
where you will be in the initial formation.
Determine which radio frequency you will
be working on. Establish codes as necessary.
Designate pyrotechnics with meanings if
appropriate. Go over any necessary hand
and arm signals or special signals you
will use.

OPERATIONS ORDER--SUMMARY

1) **SITUATION:**   Enemy Forces: Who
                                      How many
                                      Equipment
                                      Courses of action
                                      Status

                        Friendly Forces: Higher hqs
                                      Adjacent units
                                      Lower units

2) **MISSION**

3) **EXECUTION:**   General Concept of Operation

                        Sub-unit Missions

                        Coordinating Instructions

4) **SERVICE SUPPORT:** Items of Equipment

                        Ammo

                        Pyrotechnics

5) **COMMAND & SIGNAL:** Chain of Command: 1.____   2.____   3.____
                                              4.____   5.____   6.____

                        Your Location: _____

                        Frequency/Channel: _____

                        Special Signals: _____

When considering your route to the objective area, there are five aspects concerning terrain that must by considered. These assist in your determination of your SCHEME OF MANEUVER. This is planned from the assembly area through the objective.

O   Observation & Fields of Fire. Does the route provide you with good observation and fields of fire? Does it provide the same to your opponent?

K   Key Terrain. What key terrain features are in your area of operations? Will they have to be covered by men or fire to insure your success?

O   Obstacles. What obstacles will you face along the routes you consider, i.e., open areas, restricted alleys, cyclone fence, debris?

C   Cover & Concealment. Does your route offer a sufficient amount of both or either to you?

A   Avenues of Approach. Are there opponent avenues of approach into you area? Are there avenues of approach into the opponent's area?

Take each possible course of action you have as far as maneuver and then apply the five principles to that particular course. You will be able to determine by objective comparison that some aspects are better on some courses than others. Finally, you should choose the course of action that applies these principles most in your favor. Key point is that you should always try to develop at least two possible courses of action and then apply these principles.

COORDINATION TO BE EFFECTED AT THE SCENE OF AN INCIDENT

Where a building assault is anticipated, find out:

Who are you facing? Names, demeanor, previous record or history, number.
What type of weapons does he/they have?
What is their description?
Are they good shots (if they have fired)?
Are blueprints of the building available? Have they been sent for?
If blueprints are unavailable, can someone draw the floor plan of the building for you?
If decided to shut off power, gas, and water, have proper agencies been notified?
Have these agencies responded?
Is there anyone who knows the subjects available to attempt to communicate with them?
Have communications been attempted? Established? Results? Demands?
What has transpired since the first officer arrived on the scene?
What incidents led to this situation?
Are there any hostages?
Have neighboring buildings and the area in general been cleared of all innocent persons?
What are the capabilities of the Law Enforcement Agencies on the scene to render assistance if required?
What is the thickness of interior walls and the material they are constructed of?
What is the roof constructed of?
What is the disposition of LEAs on the scene?
What is the best method of gaining access to the building? Are covered and concealed routes to the house in existence? (A leader's reconnaissance of the area by the team leader of the SWAT team and his assistants will help determine this.) If not, would a helicopter enable the team to effect a successful approach? Can smoke or gas be effectively employed? Will a diversion assist in effecting entry?

Depending on the situation, the assaulting team may wish to coordinate all of the above areas or only a few. Again, depending of the situation, there may be more information required before executing a plan of attack.

CONCEALMENT	COVER

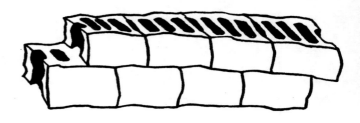

BUSHES: Can't see you but can shoot you

REINFORCED CONCRETE WALL: Can't see you, can't shoot you.

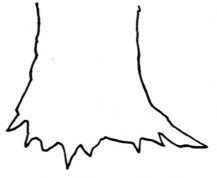

TALL GRASS: Can't see you but can shoot you.

LARGE TREE TRUNK: Can't see you, can't shoot you.

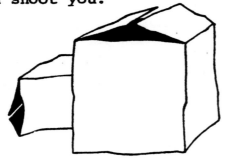

CARDBOARD BOXES/TRASH CONTAINERS: Can't see you but can shoot you.

BOULDERS: Can't see you, can't shoot you.

REMEMBER: Concealment hides you from enemy observation. Cover hides you from enemy observation <u>and</u> fire. A position that affords cover & concealment is the most desired.

CAMOUFLAGE: Observe the area you will be operating in. This will tell you what type of camouflage to use. In a building you may wish to darken your face and hands to take advantage of shadows, etc. In the woods you may wish to use earth colors and cut leaves to break up your outline.

Use soft cap (baseball type is suitable).

Camouflage face and neck.

Tape all loose equipment. You should be able to jump lightly and hear no noise.

Take all change/keys and other noisemakers out of pockets.

Tone down shiny surfaces on weapons and equipment.

Camouflage hands or wear gloves.

Remove or tape sling so that it is quiet

If deemed appropriate, paint or color the uniform to match the surrounding area.

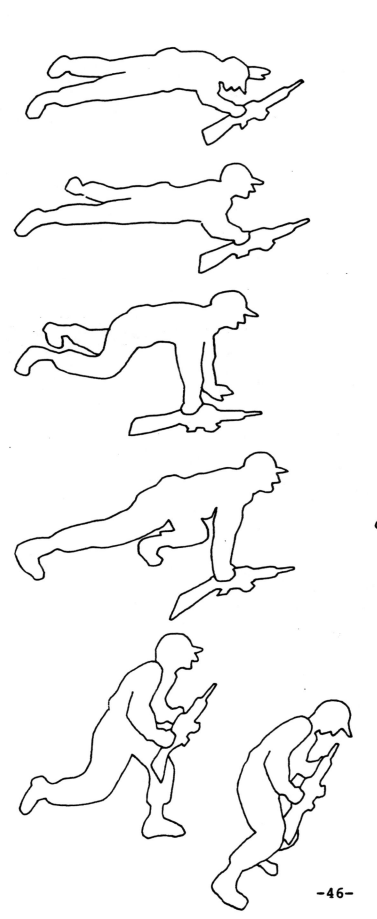

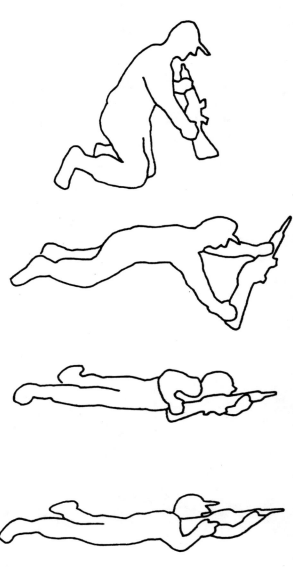

The rush is the fastest way to move from one position to another. Make sure that when you leave one position, you have cover and concealment, or concealment at the point you are rushing to. Rush no more than three seconds if you are under fire. As soon as you hit the ground, come up ready to fire.

CROSSING A WALL, LEDGE, OR FENCE

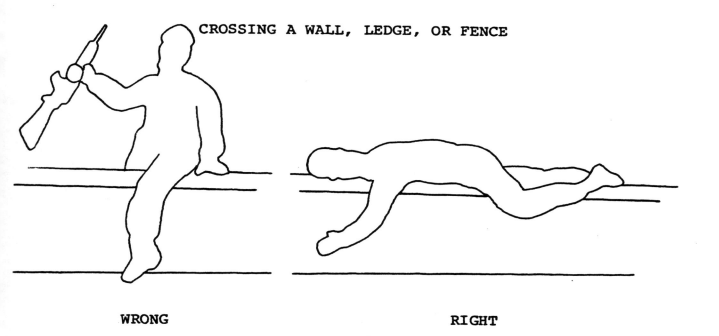

WRONG   RIGHT

CROSSING A STREET OR OPEN AREA TO ANOTHER POSITION

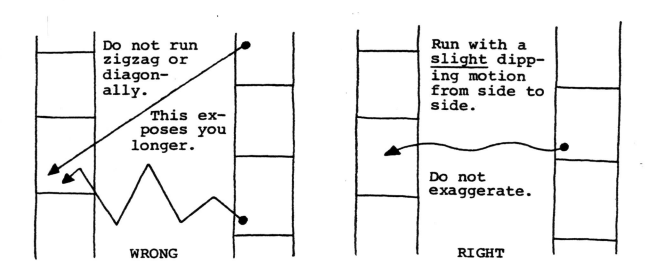

Do not run zigzag or diagonally.

This exposes you longer.

WRONG

Run with a **slight** dipping motion from side to side.

Do not exaggerate.

RIGHT

HAND AND ARM SIGNALS

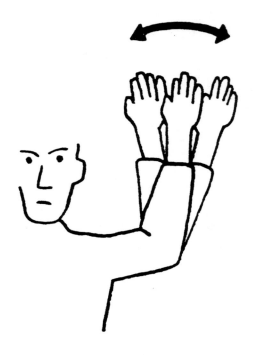

Give me your attention
or "Attention."

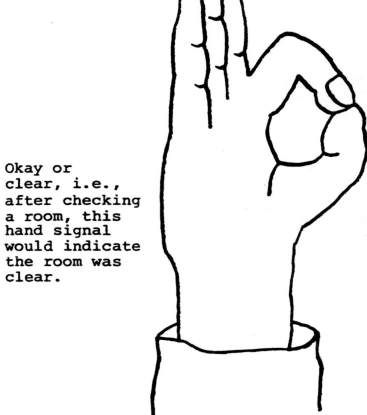

Okay or
clear, i.e.,
after checking
a room, this
hand signal
would indicate
the room was
clear.

Put on your mask, or
prepare to use gas.

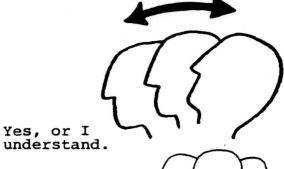

Yes, or I
understand.

No, or I do
not understand.

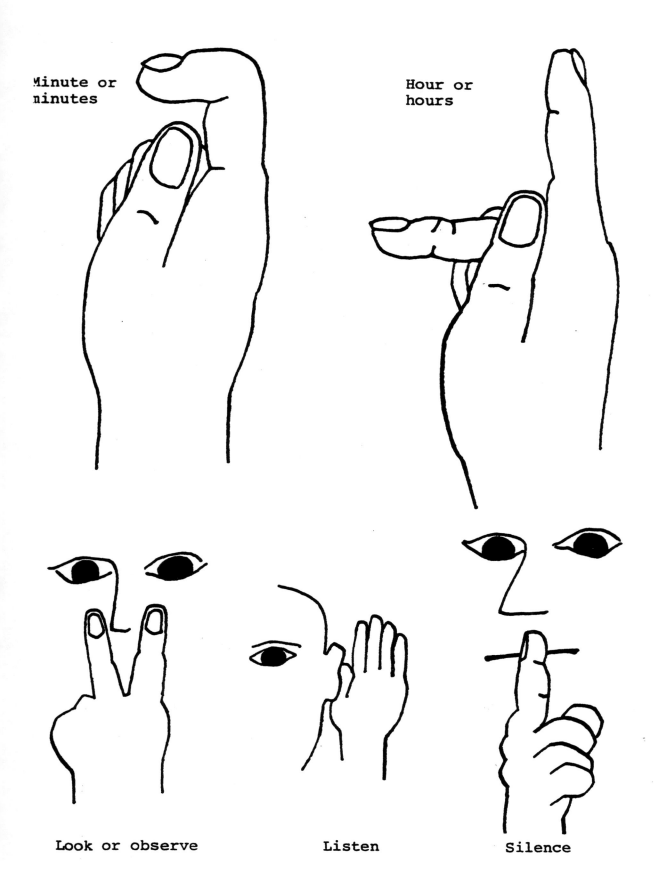

Minute or minutes

Hour or hours

Look or observe

Listen

Silence

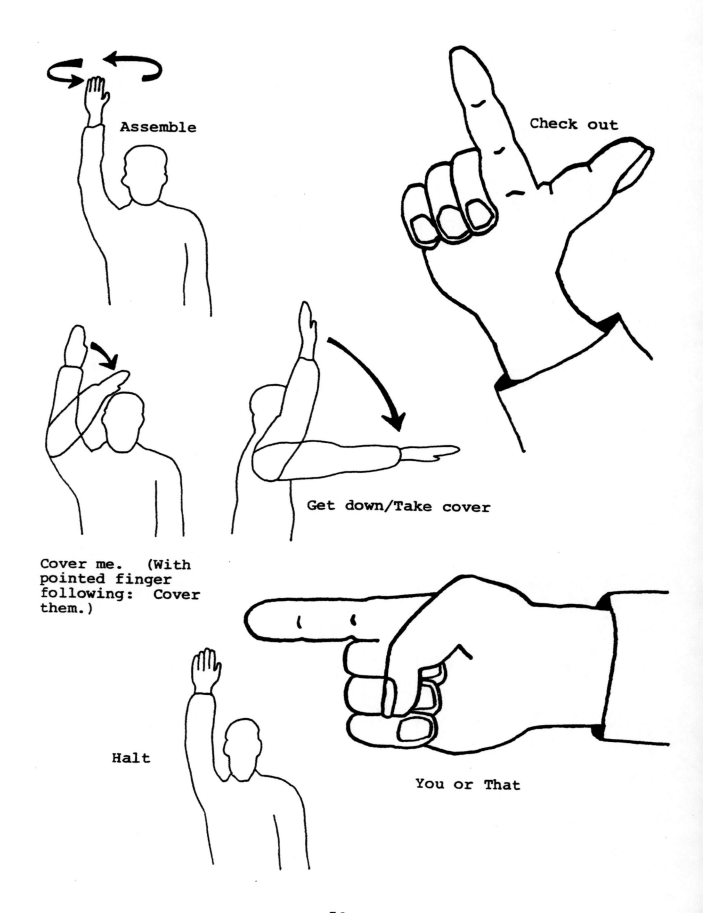

Assemble

Check out

Get down/Take cover

Cover me. (With
pointed finger
following: Cover
them.)

Halt

You or That

OBSERVING

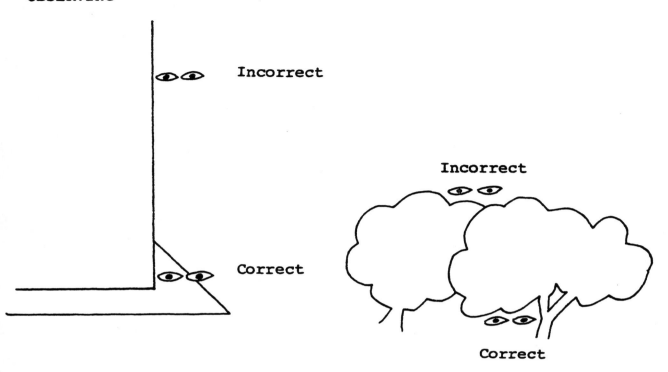

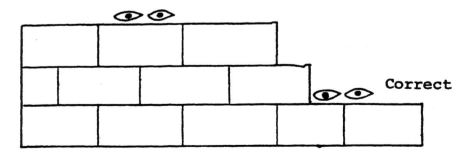

SILHOUETTING

Silhouetting yourself in an operation can lessen your chances
of survival greatly. Silhouetting is simply having your form
illuminated from behind by a light or a lighter background.
Below are some examples of silhouetting to avoid:

Silhouetting members of a rooftop against the sky, day or night.

Silhouetted through a window in the rear.

Silhouetted by car lights.

Silhouetted against a
light colored fence.

Silhouetted by a door.

MOVEMENT NEAR OBJECTIVE AREA

When passing windows on the outside of a building (or inside), insure all of you body is lower than the lowest portion of the window. The figure of the left stands an excellent chance of becoming a fatality, while the figure on the right passes the window with minimal risk.

When passing a ground level window, again you must suspect that a hostile subject is there with a weapon ready to fire. The figure on the left would almost certainly become a casualty, while the figure on the right takes a minimal risk.

MOVEMENT

When in a wooded area or building and close to the subject,
walk raising the knees fairly high, allowing the toe to touch
the ground first, and then slowly and lightly resting the rest
of your foot to the ground. Much swishing of grass or leaves
can be avoided in this manner. In a building, trip wires and
small surface obstacles can often be negotiated with safety
and no noise.

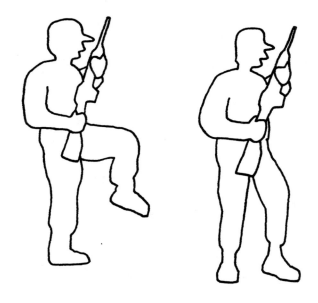

KEEP YOUR WEAPON AT THE READY (MUZZLE DOWN PREFERABLY).

FIGURE I

HALLWAYS

Hallways are extremely dangerous and should be avoided whenever possible.

If it should become necessary for your team to negotiate a hallway, do not move in the center as depicted in FIGURE I. All personnel should be agains the wall on the same side of the hallway, as in FIGURE II. Movement will be conducted by allowing two men to move ahead of the remainder of the team. They move ten to twenty feet, or doorway to doorway, then stop. The rest of the team covers this movement. Once this point element stops, they cover the movement of the remainder of the team forward.

It is difficult to avoid being silhouetted in a hallway. Movement past windows in the hall must be completed rapidly.

Lights from behind must be eliminated if at all possible. A window can be darkened with a blanket. Lights can be shut off or broken.

Rest of team waits & covers by fire if required.

FIGURE II

-55-

METHODS OF MOVING ACROSS SHORT OPEN AREAS BETWEEN BUILDINGS

Crossing the open area as
depicted in this example is
WRONG. Moving one man at a
time will alert the subject
that more may be coming. He
will probably have his weapon
trained on the open area by
the time the 2nd or 3rd
man attempts to cross.

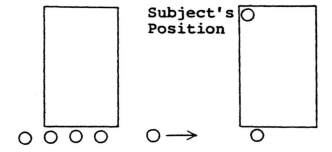

This example is correct.
After insuring a good
smoke screem is out, the
entire team crosses in a
rush. This obscures the
subject's vision and often
is so fast that he will not
be able to get off a shot.

Tm crosses in a group

This example is also correct.
All above applies except
the team crosses on line.
This cuts down the chance
of being hit from the
flank even more.

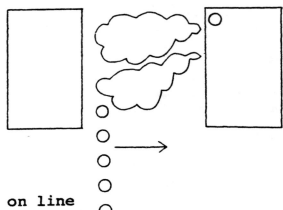

Tm crosses on line

COMMUNICATIONS AVAILABLE

VOICE: The most easily understood. Rapid and complete.
Depending on the situation may be used at all times. (A
whisper can be made softer by exhaling about one-fourth of
the breath before you speak.) In some instances you will not be
able to speak, i.e., you may wish to surprise your subject.
In the assault there will be no reason to remain silent, as the
subject will know you are present. As a rule the majority of
your talking should be done before you begin.

HAND AND ARM SIGNALS: They are extremely effective as long as
everyone knows what they mean and can see you giving them.

WHISTLES: Can be used on a limited basis. One short blast
could mean to commence the assault. One long blast could mean
to use gas, etc. You are limited in how many signals that you
could effectively use before losing track of what each meant, and
whether a certain whistle was long or short. (Not to be relied
on.)

PYROTECHNICS: The use of a different colored smoke grenade as a
signal for a particular movement or tactic is effective. Again,
you are limited in the number of colors or combination of colors
used before confusion is imminent.

RADIO: Radio is a good means of communications, however, it is
extra weight for each man to carry. It may also eliminate your
chances of obtaining surprise, should someone key the handset at
a critical time. Most people also feel that they have to use a
radio if they carry one. This often results in not being able
to get on the air because of inconsequential traffic. Where
possible, radios (with the exception of one that links the team

to higher hqs) should not be carried. Again, this does not hold true for every situation! Training your team in the proper use of radio can make it a reasonably favorable piece of equipment to carry.

MESSENGER: This is an effective way to communicate if the situation permits. Messages to be relayed by a messenger must be kept simple. There is always the possibility that a messenger may add to or detract from the message. This is not done maliciously, but is a human trait. A complicated message of any length may often be so twisted by the time it reaches the party for whom it was intended, that it is worthless. When you are under fire there may also be a high degree of risk for the messenger, and the chance that the message will never be received.

It is suggested that a combination of at least two means of communications be planned and used for each operation. If all means can be used, so much the better. All members of the team should be aware of how to use different means of communications. Your team should develop standard signals for these means and practice their use continuously.

Lack of or loss of communications will always cause a loss of control. To what degree is entirely dependent on the training status of your team.

CONTROL AND COMMUNICATIONS

Control over a group of men when marching, depending on the degree
of difficulty in the maneuvers and the level of training of the
men, can often be very difficult to maintain.

Now imagine you are controlling a group of men in exacting maneuvers where they will be using live ammunition, and someone
is trying to kill them! It is evident that this too will be
difficult, to say the least.

Control exercised by a leader is one of the factors determining
whether a mission will succeed or fail miserably. There is no
one way to exercise control that is workable for everyone. Rather,
there are control factors that if applied and practiced can be
of tremendous value.

1) Train your men as a team. Cross train them so that each man
   knows the others' jobs. Then if the leader is incapacitated
   the next in line can step in with the least amount of
   difficulty.

2) Issue clear, concise orders. If you are the leader, ask
   questions to insure each man understands perfectly. If you
   are a member receiving an order, ASK when you don't understand perfectly. Anything left in doubt will as a rule come
   to pass, leaving you at a dangerous disadvantage.

3) Follow the orders of your leader to the letter. If there is a
   problem that prohibits you from doing this, let your leader
   know IMMEDIATELY, don't wait for him to recognize the problem.

4) Be specific in orders and do not generalize.

5) Use plain, simple ENGLISH.

6) Maintain unit integrity "as much" as you possibly can. Never send one man alone to do anything.

7) In training, insert critical problems into your plans unannounced to see how you and your people react.

8) Stay away from "canned" exercises as much as possible after basic techniques have been learned.

9) Use standard Hand and Arm Signals that all your men are familiar with. Don't invent something on the spur of the moment and expect your men to know!

10) Know the capabilities and limitations of each man in your unit.

11) Know your own capabilities and limitations.

12) Demand compliance with orders as a leader.

13) TRAIN, MAKE ON THE SPOT CORRECTIONS, RETRAIN, EVALUATE, CRITIQUE, TRAIN.

14) TRAINING MUST BE TOTALLY REALISTIC AT ALL TIMES.

WEAPONS TRAINING

The weapons carried by a team must meet only two criteria:

1) They will get the job done effectively and meet the requirements of the situation, i.e., good close in, good stopping power, easy to carry, rugged, multi-shot capacity.

2) The weapon must be carried by a man or men who are experts
with that weapon, i.e., can shoot expertly with the weapon--
either hand firing ability (the man optimally should be able
to fire expertly with both hands; if this is not possible, he
should be able to hit with consistency a target firing from
the off hand or shoulder), be totally familiar with the ball-
istics of his weapon and ammunition, be adept at quick kill
(Army training of immediate pointing and firing in rapid encounter situations), and be able to conduct field maintenance
and immediate corrective action against a stoppage or misfire.

Weapons carried will vary from locality to locality, department
to department, and team to team. Again apply Rule 1.

Handguns should be considered for each man on the team in addition
to his primary weapon, whether it be rifle or shotgun. The service
revolver or pistol that the man carries on duty will more than
likely be sufficient. As such the man will be qualified with that
pistol. Whether the weapon is a .38 service revolver or a .45
caliber automatic, insure that Rule 2 applies.

Shotguns: For a close in weapon with stopping power and versatility, the shotgun is unequalled. You will have assorted shot
that can be used, from a skeet load to a deer slug. The weapon
can be used to launch grenades (with required attachments). It
is rugged, and usually operates with a relatively simple mechanical
system, negating numerous malfunctions. Pumps or Automatics will
work effectively. At least one automatic shotgun should be carried.
This is handy for the first man coming off of a rappel or Australian Crawl mission where he cannot free both hands. It is also
extremely effective for laying down cover fire for short periods
of time.

Automatic Rifles: There are a number of good auto/semi-automatics
on the market that are available for police use today. Among
these the M-16, AR-15, M-1 or M-2 Carbine seem most appropriate.
The main reason is the firepower available, weight, and ammunition
available. (Is some locales .30 caliber carbine ammunition is
scarce. The stopping power of the .223 in many cases is under-
estimated. Other factors to be considered are recoil (very little
with the above), ability to control semi or auto firing, and
amount of ammunition that can be carried without becoming overly
cumbersome.

Sniper Rifles: Numerous choices are again available. The type of situation expected most will dictate the type of weapon to carry. The most professional guidance to be given here is that whether the weapon is a 30.06, .223, .222, .243 or whatever, the marksman is the key. This individual must be the best shot available. He must have a love for firing. He must practice, practice, practice. His practice must not be limited to bulls-eye targets from a bench rest, but should include combat firing positions at targets such as subjects with a hostage, groups of targets, and obscured targets. He should fire from different angles than straight on. He should engage targets through glass window panes of varying thicknesses. Have him fire under varying climatic and light conditions. Have him fire after participating in strenuous physical exercise.

PYROTECHNICS

The use of pyrotechnics (smoke, gas, and simulators basically, with flare and star clusters) can be of value to the SWAT team in the accomplishment of a given mission, when used correctly. When used improperly they can be a hindrance and possibly disastrous.

Smoke: Smoke is often used to conceal friendly movement from the subjects. Thrown between the subject's position and the friendly forces, a good smoke screen will completely obscure the friendly team's activities. It will also obscure the subject's position. Thrown on the subject's position, it will obscure his vision of friendly activities, yet allow the friendly forces to maintain vision of the subject's position. (Not the subject himself, but his position.) Smoke can be used to conceal movement across open areas. It may be used to conceal movement forward or backward when under fire or "pinned down." It may be used as a signal. Some types of smoke may not dissipate for long periods of time. In enclosed areas, smoke will make the control of a friendly team more difficult. In open areas, wind may carry smoke in the wrong direction or thin it rapidly. Wind direction and speed must be considered in using smoke outdoors.

Gas: Gas, like smoke, can be a boon or a curse. When used in an enclosed area it may linger for long periods of time. Outdoors it may be blown away before its effects are useful. If you plan to rush a building immediately after using gas, you will be required to wear a mask. All members of a team should attempt to run a fair distance with a mask on, or better yet, attempt to fire accurately. It is difficult, to say the least. In no way do I berate the potential of gas. There are numerous situations where it could be considered essential. Learn to operate in your masks. Use gas sparingly unless all conditions are right for its use. Be aware of the fact that some gas projectiles will burn while others will explode. Be prepared for the eventuality of a fire. Be prepared for a shift in wind direction which can move the gas out of the objective area. Be prepared for a cannister grenade to be thrown back at you. If you use cannister grenades try to take advantage of wind direction. If the wind is blowing toward the subject's position, throw the grenade slightly in front of the position. For him to kick it away or throw it back, he will have to expose himself. If it is blowing from behind his position, throw the gas behind him. HAVE YOUR MASKS READY. The same applies to the wind blowing right or left. Throw the grenade upwind of his position and you will normally have the desired results.

Simulators: These are small cylindrical grenades weighing about one-eighth lb. There is no metal casing, the grenade is wrapped in a paper mache type material. There is no fragmentation. This grenade is called a simulator because it simulates an artillery round exploding. A pull string is jerked and the grenade is thrown on or near the enemy position. The jerking of the string ignites a delayed fuse, which reaches the main charge (nearly one-eighth lb. of TNT) in five to six seconds, exploding with a tremendous concussion force. In a small room with the windows and doors closed, the concussion would knock the windows out of the frames. And certainly shake up an occupant. There is some danger of fire. A recommended procedure for a team is to throw one of these into a room and close the door. If the subject remains inside, he is warned that more will come. If there is still no action on his part to surrender, three or four are thrown on his position in the room (this can be determined by the use of mirrors). Upon detonation an immediate assault is launched. He will usually throw out his weapon after the first one in.

Fuzees, Star Clusters, and Flares: These can provide excellent signals for team use. They are also effective in illuminating areas of darkness.

ENTERING A BUILDING

The SWAT team assigned the mission of clearing a building will
be concerned as to the proper methods available to entering the
building. Going into an unfamiliar place is dangerous to say
the least; not knowing other means than the door is suicide.
THE FOLLOWING ARE ACCEPTABLE METHODS OF ENTERING BUILDINGS AND HAVE
BEEN USED IN ACTUAL SITUATIONS.

Grappling hook to the top floor: A team member will throw a
grappling hook through one of the top floor windows (preferably
away from the suspect's position). The member then climbs to
the window. If he is reasonably sure that the room is empty,
he enters, immediately rolling in over the ledge. If there is
doubt as to the occupancy of that room, he may tie off on the rope
and use his mirror to quickly survey the interior of the room.
Appropriate action such as gas, simulators, or weapons fire
(depending on departmental policy) may be called for from the
tied off position. Once he has cleared the room, the remainder
of his team climbs the rope (knotted to make climbing easier
and pulled to a corner of the window for support and ease of
entry) and joins him; from here they will continue with their
mission.

Chopping a hole in the roof: If access to the roof is available,
and all other means of entering the building are unfeasible, you
may be required to cut your way through the roof (or any other
part of the building; the roof serves only as an example).
Axes, sledge hammers, and pry bars are best for this. The major
disadvantage is that if you are assaulting a relatively small
building, the hostile persons will hear you. Numerous large
caliber weapons could easily pierce most roofs. If the hostiles
have such weapons, they may indiscriminately fire through the
roof on your team. If the building is large (department store),
there may be a skylight, and even if there isn't, the chances
of the hostiles hearing your activities are reduced. It is normally better to enter above your suspects. It is easier for you
to fight down. Also, if you fight towards the upper floors, you
allow the hostiles no way out. A cornered rat fights a dev-
astating fight.

Rappelling from the roof to an upper window: If you are able to
get to the roof (helicopter, ladder, rope) you may wish to consider
rappelling from the roof to an upper floor window. Once you
lower yourself to the window desired, all activities become the

same as if you had climbed up with a grappling hook (entering, observing, smoke, gas, simulators, weapons fire, according to departmental policy). Again, you try to enter above the hostiles and drive them down to the streets. (Remember there are police officers all around the building.)

Sewers, vents, and other pipes: Especially in larger buildings. These means of access can be determined by studying blueprints, or consulting building personnel. Crawl spaces may be used if available.

Explosives: (Depending on departmental policy.) Explosives can be an effective means of gaining access to a building. Properly trained demolition personnel can blow small holes in walls of buildings and rooms to gain access. This is called mouseholing. Caution must be exercised as to the situation, training level of the demolition man, and potential damages that might occur.

Doors and windows: Discussed in other sections of the manual.

Armored Vehicle: The armored vehicle can get a team into a building with relative safety. If it can be used effectively, it should be contemplated.

General: In many cases, procedures may be somewhat similar in each type of entry. Gas, smoke, and simulators may be planned and used as a preparation for each entry. SWAT units should practice each type of entry discussed within their capability, and be prepared for the eventual use of any.

ROOM CLEARING

The most dangerous part of room clearing is without a doubt getting into the room and establishing a foothold.

1) Team will organize itself as indicated in FIGURE I. Inspect the door visually for any signs of trip wires or other indications of boobytrapping. Having done this (thoroughly), check to see if the door opens in or out. If it opens in, the man as in FIGURE I grasps the knob, turns slightly, and kicks inward.

(He does not stand in front of the door and kick, but rather stays to the side.) If the door opens outwardly, a line can be attached to the knob, it can be turned and then pulled from the opposite side of the knob. Again, no one is exposed. If the door is locked, a pry bar or sledge may be required. Only in dire situations should a unit attempt to shoot the lock out of a door. This is because you do not know what or who could be behind it.

2) Once the door is open, the men nearest the door on opposite sides use the mirrors attached to the butts of their weapons to observe inside. They do not expose any part of their bodies, i.e., fingers, hands, feet, knees. The room is searched from top to bottom and from corner to corner. Those observing must describe the inside of the room to those providing security, as everyone may be required to enter the room. Some areas may be difficult to observe, but by moving the weapons around or allowing the opposite mirror man to look in your mirror you will be able to see the entire room. If the suspect is located, you may be able to talk him out; it's a tremendous surprise for him to know that you can see him. You may use smoke, gas, or simulators accurately, without ever having exposed yourself. You may (depending on departmental policy) take this man out by sticking just the barrel of your weapon around the corner and allowing a mirror man to direct your fire. Normally the application will be Talk, Smoke, Gas, Simulators, and finally, Weapons Fire or Assault.

3) Assuming you observe the room and see no one, you will want to enter it and make a thorough search. In our example the #2 and #5 men enter the room first (except in FIGURE VI, where the #2, #5. #1, and #4 men enter the room together). The first man in the room moves to the wall by the door and attempts to find cover. If none is available he makes himself the smallest target possible by squatting, kneeling, or lying down. The next man in the door in FIGURE IV moves through the room, searching under the cover of the first man in. In FIGURE V, the #2 and #5 men enter and hug the wall near the door on opposite sides of the opening. They then move around the room, staying along the walls. The mirror men move into the doorway to support with fire if required. In FIGURE VI, the #1, #4, #3, and #5 men enter the room and move along the walls of the room until it has been searched. The #3 and #6 men move to the entrance of the room to provide cover fire if required.

When moving in a room, avoid windows or lights that will silhouette you.

Move in a crouch position with your weapon at the ready.

Treat closets as you would another room until you are sure they are cleared.

Take your time. Observe ten times for every move you make.

Touch nothing that does not have to be touched. Boobytraps!

Insure that while one man is moving, another is able to cover him.

FIGURE I

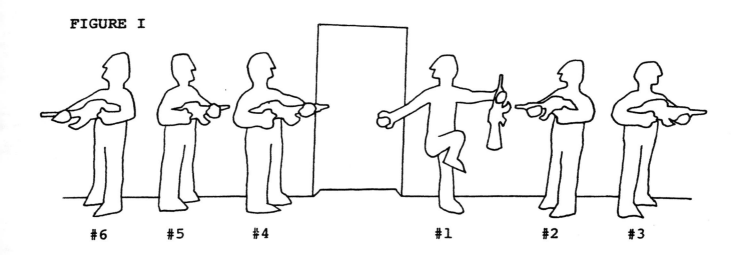

#6   #5   #4   #1   #2   #3

FIGURE II

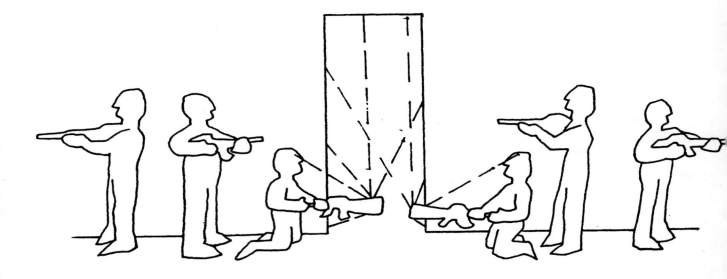

NOTE: Expose no part of your body. Insure the team maintains good security for mirror men.

FIGURE III

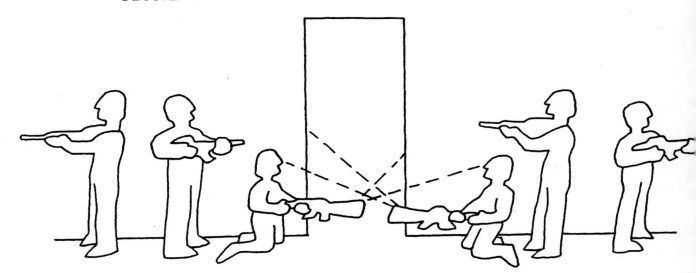

NOTE: Look at room with mirror while standing, kneeling and lying down. Each position gives a different view of the room. Allow the man opposite you to look in and direct your mirror. This will give you a better picture of the room.

FIGURE IV

NOTE: Search must be thorough, covering entire room.

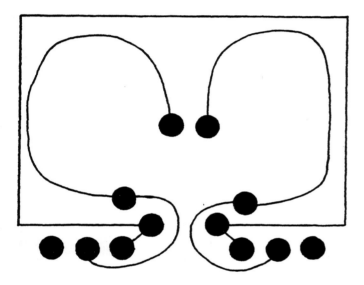

FIGURE V

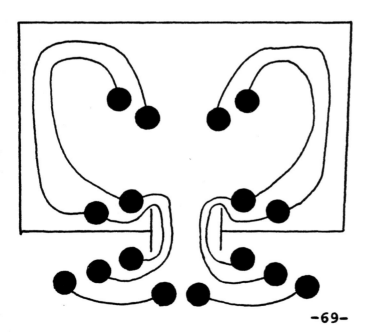

FIGURE VI

This is usually used for a larger room or when many rooms lead off the primary one, requiring continuous movement from one room into another.

METHODS OF ENTRY

Member with a grappling hook,
standing as close to the building
as possible, throws hook through
top window. NOTE: The member
throwing the hook must be
covered by fire support
at all times.

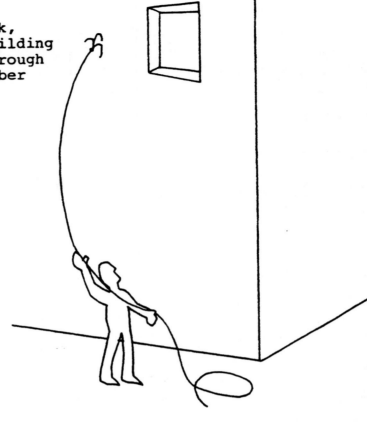

Once hook is through
window it is pulled
to one corner and
set (pulled hard) to
insure it will hold.

Inside view
of proper
hook posit-
ioning.

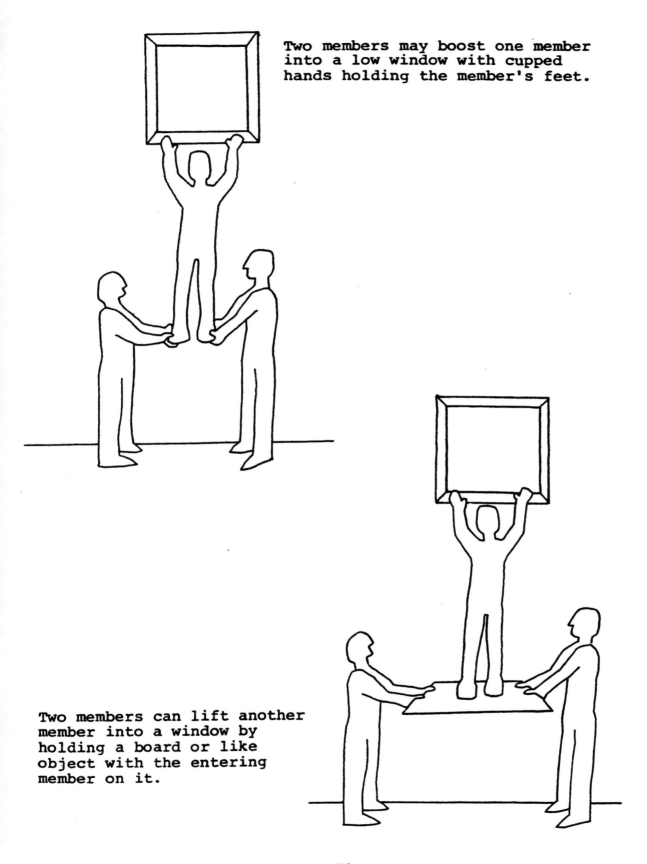

Two members may boost one member
into a low window with cupped
hands holding the member's feet.

Two members can lift another
member into a window by
holding a board or like
object with the entering
member on it.

ADDITIONAL MEANS OF GAINING ACCESS TO DOORS AND WINDOWS

When approached with breaking glass to obtain entry to a building or room, use an axe or the butt of your weapon, striking the glass at the top and then striking low. This

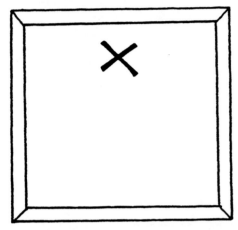

will negate the possibility of glass from the upper portion of the window fall-ing on the person trying to gain entrance. If the glass is mesh, use the blade of an axe to cut around the entire window frame.

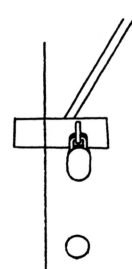

A door locked with a hasp and padlock can be entered with little difficulty. The hasp can be pried out of the frame or the lock can be broken with the aid of an axe or heavy hammer.

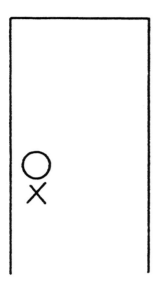

If confronted with a door that opens to the inside, use the twenty lb. sledge hammer and strike the door just below the door knob with a hard blow. In most cases this will break the door jamb and the lock. If this fails the first time, it may be continued until the door is opened.

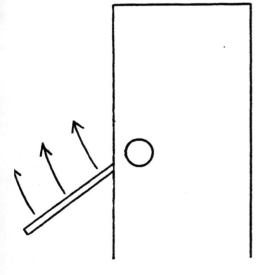

If a door opens out, insert a heavy pry bar (narrow end) between the door and the jamb, approximately where the lock enters the jamb. Apply pressure away from the door as illustrated (left). In the event it is difficult to insert the pry bar between the door and the jamb, drive it in with a hammer.

Opening a door that swings out to open can be accomplished with
relative safety as in the example below. The man nearest the door
on the right throws the end of a piece of rope across the door
to the man on the near left. The man on the left fixes a slip
knot in the rope and attaches it to the door knob. The man on
the left then turns the knob quickly and withdraws his hand.
He immediately regains his weapon and stands by. The man on
the right then pulls the door open.

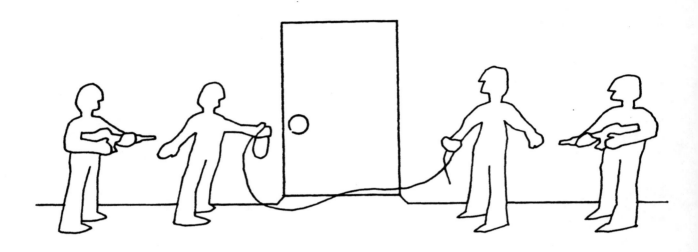

It must be noted that at no time is any person in the team left
uncovered throughout this process. The room may then be checked
with mirrors or assaulted immediately if necessary.

A variation to opening a door that swings out or in is to place
a marksman in front of the door <u>behind cover.</u> The door is pulled
or pushed open <u>fast.</u> The marksman will have a clear shot at
anything in the center of the room, and from his covered position
will be relatively safe. NOTE: He must be prepared to fire
instantly.

All other team members will be prepared to cover if necessary and
follow up on the information that the marksman will be able to
give them due to his position.

THE MIRROR

One extremely important item of equipment for any team is a
mirror/mirrors. Convex mirrors (diagram below) can give a team
a tremendous advantage over their subjects in any type of
operation.

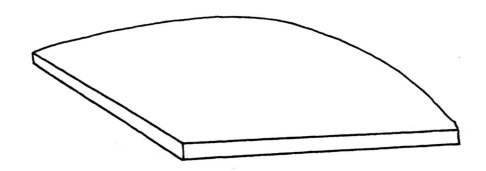

The actual uses of the mirror are explained in the next few
pages. A question may be asked after reading them such as,
"What happens if the guy shoots my mirror?" The answer is,
you buy a new one, and thank God it wasn't your head.

If you should use the mirror and spot your subject in a position
where he has good cover, and you need for him to move to get your
mission accomplished, you may say something to the effect, "There
he is in the corner behind that desk. Send Smith down the wall
and have him fire a few shots through the wall. I'll direct
his fire."

This will have an unnerving effect on the subject; one, you can
see him, and two, you will be able to direct fire on his position.

MIRROR USE

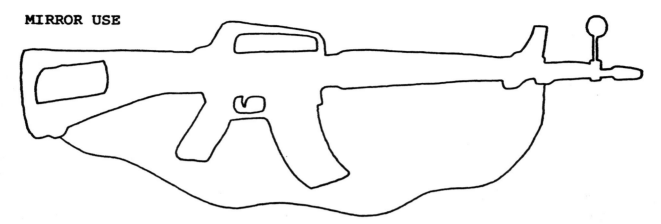

Example of mirror attached to the stock or barrel of an M16
rifle. Mirrors can be attached to the stock or barrel of any
team weapon. Shotguns are normally longer than the M16 and
can give more reach for viewing. When not using the mirror,
put an athletic knee pad (dyed black) over it. This protects
the mirror from breakage, eliminates unwanted reflection of
light, and does not impair firing the weapon. NOTE: Knee pad
is used on stock-mounted mirror only.

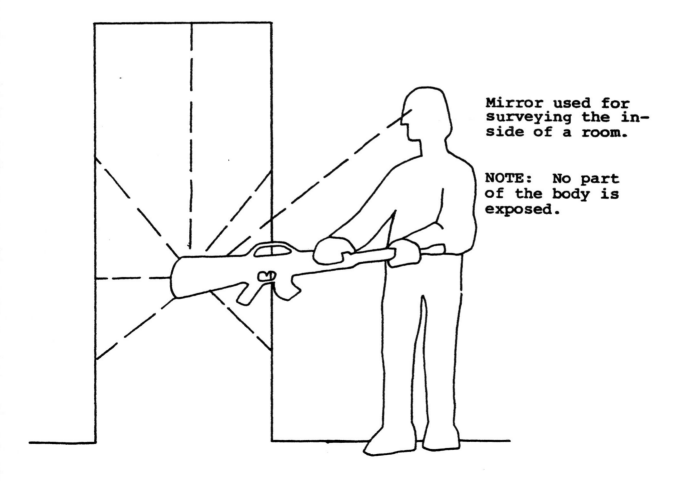

Mirror used for
surveying the in-
side of a room.

NOTE: No part
of the body is
exposed.

On a landing, by lying flat on his back, a man can observe the entire stairwell below.

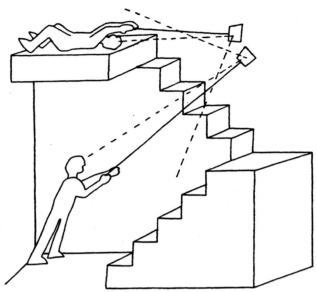

By remaining under an overhang on a stairwell, a man can see above him to insure the stairs.

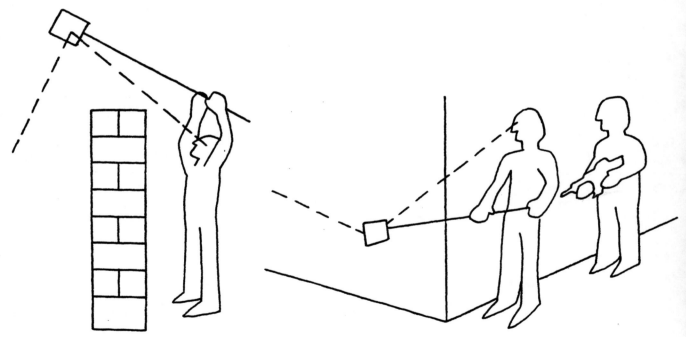

The mirror is effective for observing over walls or fences. it enables a member to observe into a building through an outside window without exposing himself or entering the building.

In this example the member is able to observe around a corner without exposing any part of his body. NOTE: Another team member must be positioned where he can provide immediate fire support.

CLEARING OF AN ENCLOSED OR STRAIGHT STAIRWELL (STAIRS DARK)

Utilizing proper principles of Fire Support, Movement, and Teamwork, negotiating an enclosed stairwell/straight stairwell can be accomplished with a greatly reduced degree of danger.

1) It first becomes very clear that the base of the stairwell must be totally secure. This involves a search and clearing operation to void the area of or identify any hostile persons or boobytraps.

2) Having accomplished this, security must be placed on both sides of the base of the stairwell. There may be times when both sides will not be tenable for your use. In these cases use only one side on which to station your personnel, but be able to cover the other with observation and fire.

3) After you have cleared the base of the stairs, personnel should be positioned as indicated in FIGURE I. Note that the men farthest away from the base of the stairs provide security to the sides.

| Security to Side | Assault Team | Illumination & Observation Team | Security to Side |

NOTE: At no time until prepared to assault does anyone expose himself to the opening at the base of the stairs, or until stairs have been observed and cleared. To get personnel across the opening to the other side, you may have to have them use another entrance to the building, or use your mirrors and flashlights to insure that the steps are clear.

4) The two inner men on one side of the base of the stairs will observe and illuminate the stairwell, while the two inner men on the other side of the base stand by to provide fire support if required. On the side that has been assigned the task of illuminating and observing the stairs, one man using an elbow flashlight extends only the light around the corner of the stairwell opening and illuminates the staircase. The other man assigned the task of observing the stairwell extends his rifle butt with mirror attached around the side of the opening and observes the stairwell. The man with the mirror will have to direct the man with the light to raise, lower, or traverse the beam of light; a slow, systematic search from the bottom step up must be made in this manner. See FIGURES II & III.

FIGURE II

NOTE: The visual search is accomplished with the elbow flashlight and mirror affixed to the stock of a shotgun or rifle. At no time does a man expose himself or any part of his body to the opening.

FIGURE III

NOTE: The light has covered from the bottom step to the top of the stairwell in systematic sweeps. At this time the observer will give the assault team the go-ahead if the stairs are clear.

5) Upon completion of the visual search, the two security men
   not assigned the mission of observing the stairwell prepare
   to move onto the stairs. If there is an opening at the top
   of the stairs on one side, the two men who negotiate the stairs
   should stay as close to the wall as possible on that side
   as they climb. If there is a "T" at the top of the stairs
   (an opening on both sides), either side of the wall may be
   "hugged." If you have an idea that the person you are after
   is off to one specific side at the top of the stairs, stay
   against that wall. The reason for this is that for the person
   to shoot you he must expose himself or a portion of his body.
   See FIGURES IV & V.

FIGURE IV

NOTE: As soon as the assault team is on the stairs, the
original observer and man with flashlight cease functioning
in that capacity.

FIGURE V

Side view of assault moving up the stairs.

6) The first man on the steps must have a shotgun, which he carries pointed at the opening at the top of the stairs. He must be ready to fire instantly, at a pistol, a hand, a face, or the barrel of a rifle. The second man will carry a handgun and a flashlight to further illuminate the area.

NOTE: Those personnel originally assigned the task of illumination of the stairs and observation continue to do so until the assault team is on the stairs. The observer with the mirror will be the man to give the assault team the signal to move onto the stairs (when he is sure that they are clear). The second man will be as close to the rear of the first man as possible. He will have his handgun extended over the shoulder (the shoulder closest to the wall) of the first man. In his other hand (held well away from the body and somewhat to the front) he will hold the flashlight to provide continuous illumination.

At no time must observation on the stairs be lost. This includes the time it takes for the assault team to get on them. Both men will proceed to the top of the stairs near the opening. Once the assault team has got on the stairs, a man from the original illumination and observation group will direct his weapon up the stairs for additional support. A rifle, NOT A SHOTGUN. Once the top of the stairs is reached, normal room clearing techniques are used. See FIGURES VI & VII. If the stairs are lighted, flashlights will not be needed.

FIGURE VI

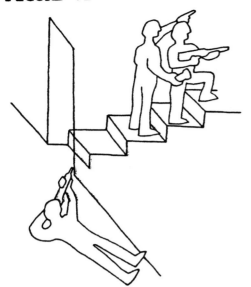

NOTE: Man from the Observing & Illumination Team now provides additional cover with a rifle from the base of the stairs.

Assault Team at top of stairs ready to continue mission.

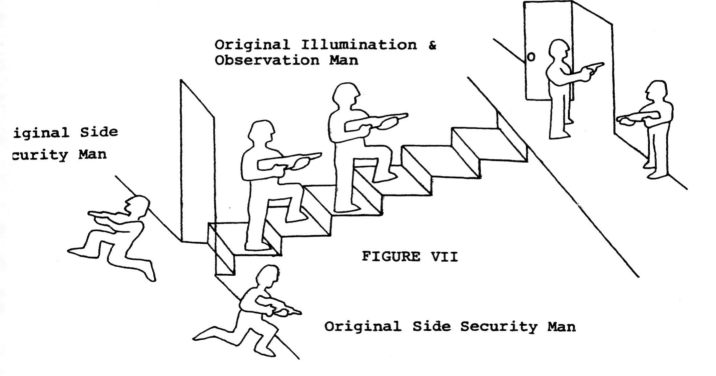

Original Illumination & Observation Man

iginal Side
curity Man

FIGURE VII

Original Side Security Man

NOTE: As the top of the stairs is secured the remainder of the team or a designated part joins the assault team; from here they continue with their mission. The original Side Security men may be left at the base of the stairs to provide security, or be replaced by support personnel and rejoin their team.

Throwing a grenade up stairs may be
necessary. If at all possible
this should be avoided unless the
top of the stairs opens into a
large open area, or you are
absolutely sure there are no
obstructions.
Due to their
rounded or
cylindrical
shape,
grenades have a
tendency to roll,
and can easily
roll back down
the stairs
onto your
posit-
ion.

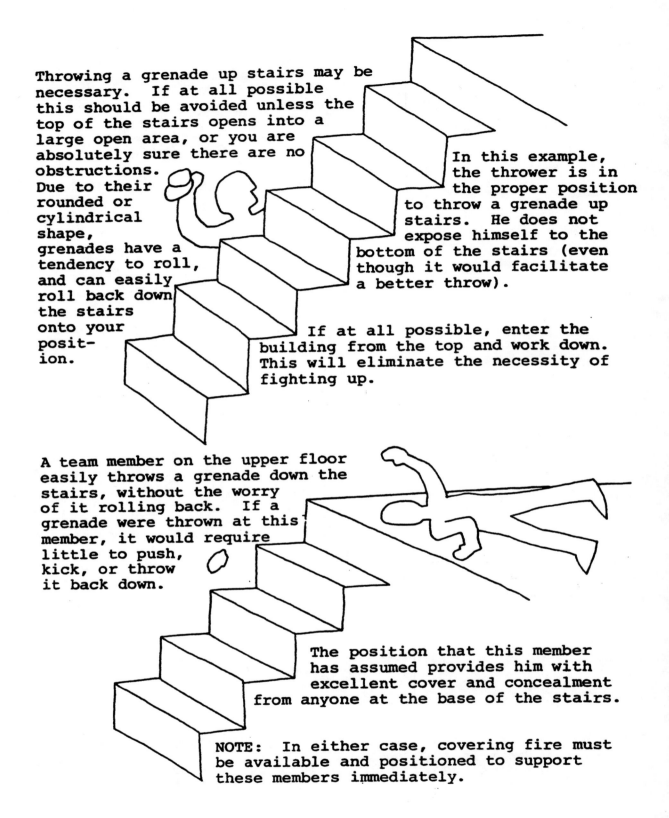

In this example,
the thrower is in
the proper position
to throw a grenade up
stairs. He does not
expose himself to the
bottom of the stairs (even
though it would facilitate
a better throw).

If at all possible, enter the
building from the top and work down.
This will eliminate the necessity of
fighting up.

A team member on the upper floor
easily throws a grenade down the
stairs, without the worry
of it rolling back. If a
grenade were thrown at this
member, it would require
little to push,
kick, or throw
it back down.

The position that this member
has assumed provides him with
excellent cover and concealment
from anyone at the base of the stairs.

NOTE: In either case, covering fire must
be available and positioned to support
these members immediately.

CLEARING THE WINDING STAIRWELL

Negotiating a winding stairwell is a dangerous operation, regardless of the method employed by the clearing unit. The following method as described will offer a distinct advantage to the team that has been assigned this task.

The first objective in the clearing of the winding stairwell is to insure that the base of the stairwell is secure. Once this is accomplished, you are ready to begin the ascent. (FIGURE I).

1) Number 1 and 2 men move into the stairwell base area. Number 1 man has the responsibility of clearing the upper portion (overhang) with the mirror attached to his weapon while #2 man provides cover. (FIGURES II, III & IV).

2) When #1 man is satisfied that the top of the stairwell is clear, he will notify the team leader who will then position #3 and 4 men at the base of the stairs where they can fire up if the need arises. Number 1 man must never lose visual contact with the top of the stairs while people are moving into positions. (FIGURES V & VI).

3) When the #3 and 4 men are in position the #1 man moves his mirror so that the intermediate landing can be observed by the #3 or 4 man. This is imperative, as the intermediate landing is a primary danger area. The #1 man will normally not be able to observe this area with the mirror, and it is for this reason that the #3 or 4 man must observe. (FIGURE VII).

4) When it is ascertained that the stairs are clear, the #2 and 5 men will prepare to move up. The #1 man will give the all clear (he is constantly observing with his mirror). Whe the all clear is given, the #2 and 5 men move up the steps backwards with their weapons ready to fire. Each man will cover one half of the top of the next landing (left to center, and center to right). (FIGURES VIII & IX).

5) As soon as the #2 and 5 men are in position where they can cover the entire top floor (landing), the #1 man moves up the stairs to provide additional cover. The #6 man takes the #1 man's place that was vacated. Number 3 and 4 men move up the stairs on command. (FIGURES X & XI).

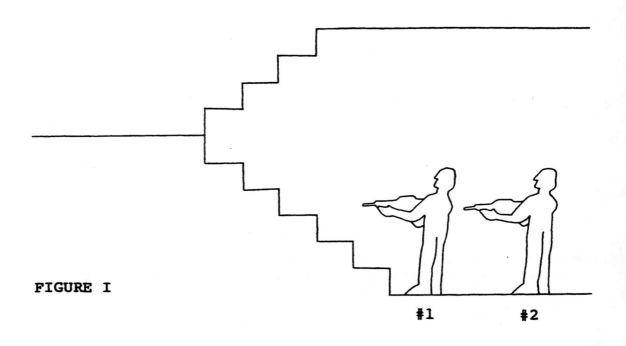

FIGURE I

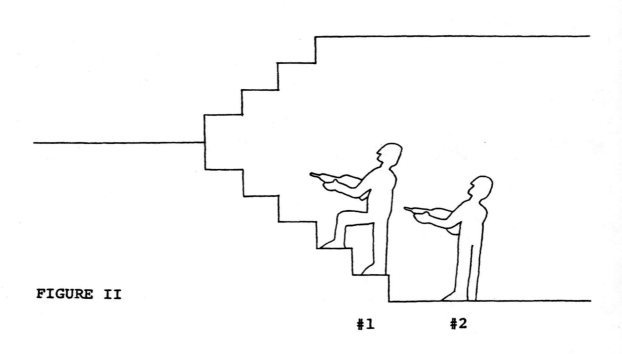

FIGURE II

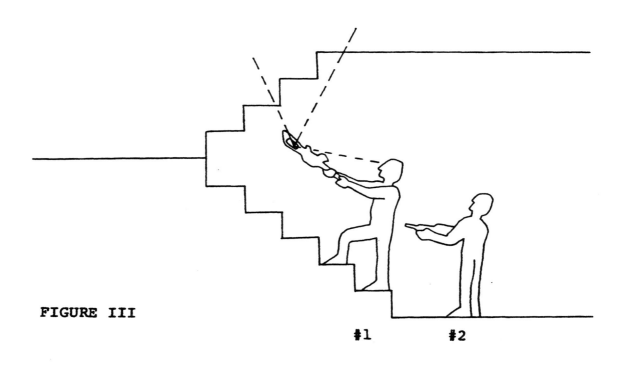

FIGURE III

#1   #2

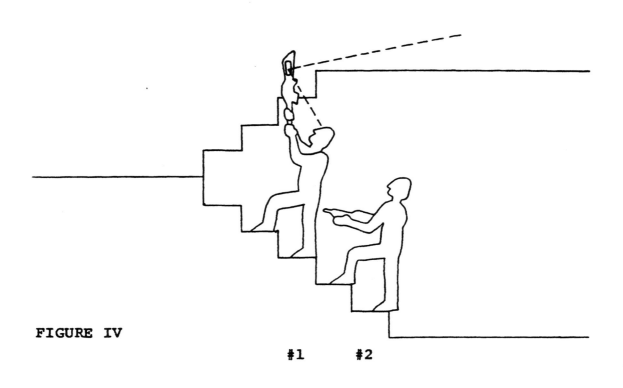

FIGURE IV

#1   #2

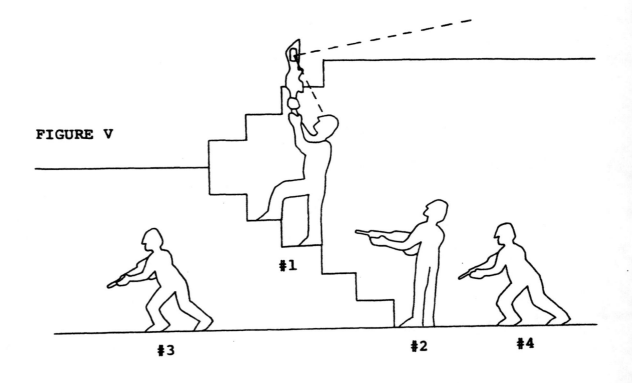

FIGURE V

#1

#3

#2

#4

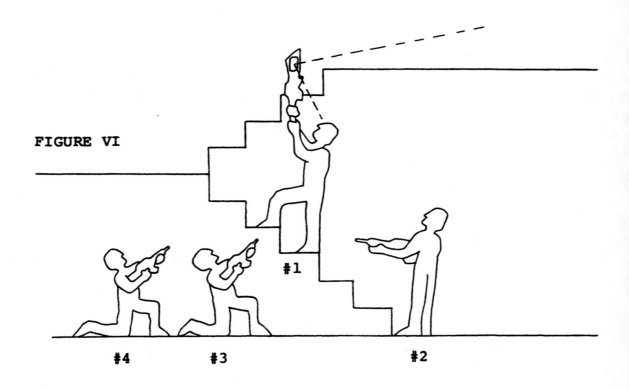

FIGURE VI

#1

#4

#3

#2

FIGURE VII

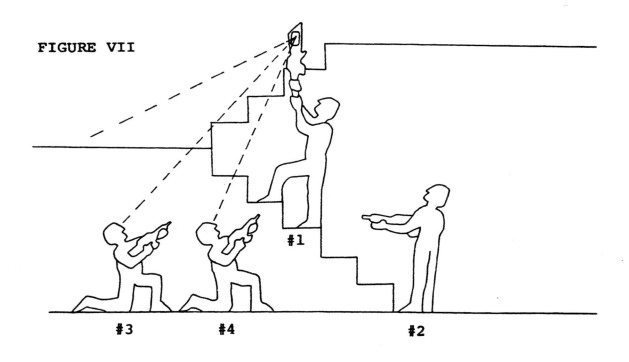

#1

#3   #4   #2

FIGURE VIII

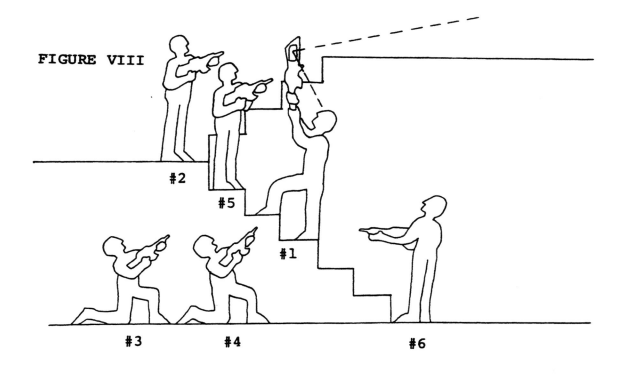

#2

#5

#1

#3   #4   #6

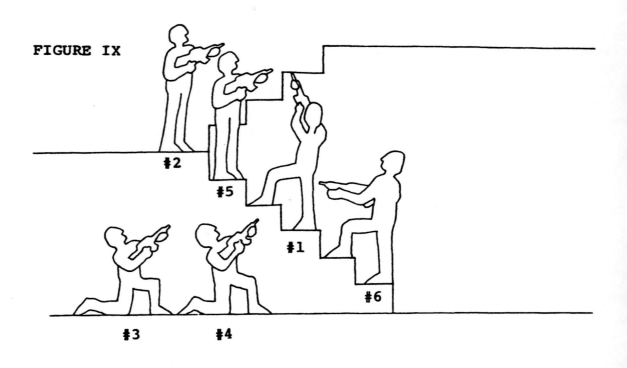

FIGURE IX

#2 #5 #1 #6 #3 #4

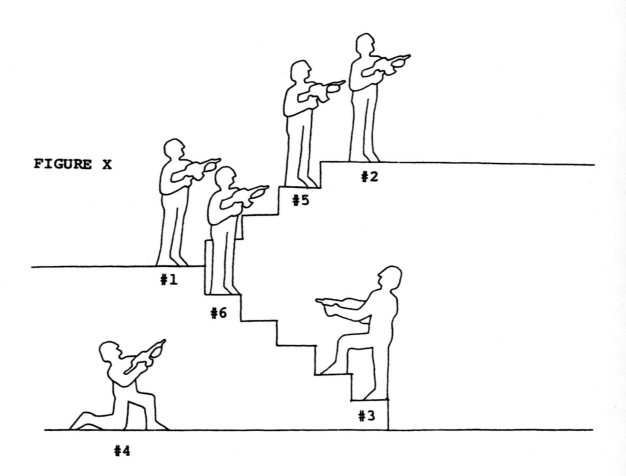

FIGURE X

#1 #5 #2 #6 #3 #4

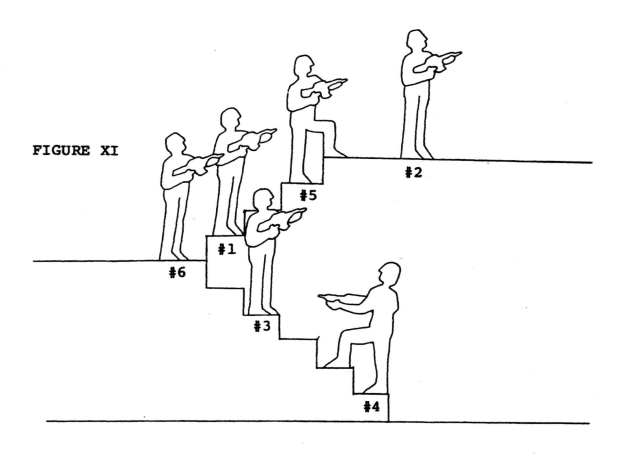

FIGURE XI

#6 #1 #3 #5 #2 #4

LARGE BUILDING CLEARING OPERATIONS

In many ways clearing a large building, such as a factory or
department store, resembles the clearing of an outdoor area.
You must maintain maximum dispersion, security by observation
(front, sides, rear, and up), and you must be prepared to initiate
battle drill in a fraction of a second. It is suggested that
when conducting large building clearing operations, teams assume
a bounding overwatch posture. Remember this exposes the least
amount of personnel forward who are still an integral team.
It also provides a fixed position of support fire while one
team is moving (on an alternating basis between teams) so that
each team has 100 percent support at all times. Cover and
Concealment must be used to a maximum. Listening halts must be
taken very often for relatively long periods of time, in attempts
to locate the hostiles before they locate you. Upon locating
the hostiles, immediate action must be taken to fix them in position. Contact must not be lost. A well prepared hostile will
more than likely get off one well aimed shot at your team before
you locate him. If allowed to move out of the area and establish
another position, he will get another well aimed shot at you before
you locate him again, more likely than not. Once the hostile
position is fixed and the hostile is isolated and contained,
departmental policy will dictate what courses of action will
be taken next. Talking, use of smoke or gas, use of simulators,
assault, or engagement by sniper for a one shot kill. IT MUST
BE STRESSED, personnel must remain alert at all times, noise must
be kept to an absolute minimum, maximum use of cover must be
ordered and enforced, observation must be continuous, and personnel must be prepared to react immediately. A rifle and
shotgun should be kept well forward.

In a department store there is always a chance of innocent persons
being caught up in the situation. The best way to deal with

those whose identity is uncertain is to either evacuate under guard or secure them in an area inside the store under guard. They must always be searched. In a multi-level store, after each floor is searched, police from the cordon should be brought in to secure it so the team may continue to the next floor.

TIPS

Move slowly, observe ten times before moving once.

Maintain dispersion.

Maintain weapons at the ready.

Keep a rifle and a shotgun forward.

Utilize all available cover and concealment.

Watch for innocent civilians (especially in a department store).

The best way to deal with those that cannot be identified as innocents is to handcuff them and establish identity afterward. After any particular floor is secured, police from the cordon should be brought in to secure it. This applies to stairwells also.

USE COMMON SENSE.

THINK.

LARGE BUILDING OPERATIONS

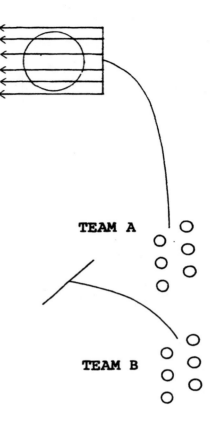

OBJECTIVE

Rear team provides fire support
while lead team maneuvers on
line oriented with the objective.
Lead team may make the assault.

Desirable only if there is no
route for the rear team to use
to maneuver against the objective. Use smoke, gas, and simulators liberally.

TEAM A

TEAM B

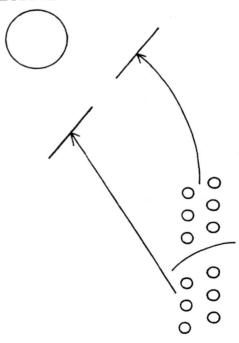

OBJECTIVE

Both teams come on line oriented
on the objective. All conduct
combined assault maneuver.

Used only when there is no route
anywhere to the objective. It is
least desirable. Use smoke, gas,
and simulators liberally.

LARGE BUILDING OPERATIONS

Rear team disengages from squad and moves along far wall by way of a concealed or covered route to a position near the objective and deploys. Front team continues movement forward to a similar position. Forces opponent to fight in two different directions. Either team may assault. Each team provides its own fire support until final assault.

Desirable when covered route is available to rear team, and front team has no acceptable position to support from. Use smoke, gas, and simulators liberally.

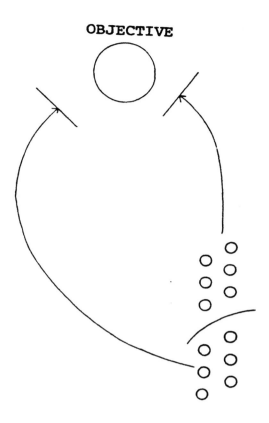

Front team has good support position. Used when rear team has a viable route. Most desirable because front team will likely know the location of enemy and be able to provide good support fire. Rear team will not be engaged initially, and will retain freedom of movement as a unit against the opponent.

OBJECTIVE

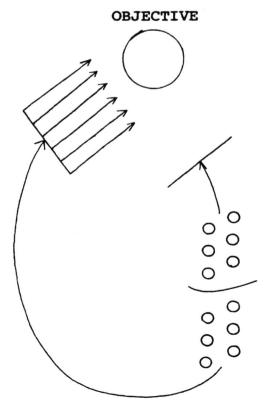

BARRICADED PERSONS

The term "barricaded persons" encompasses any person or persons who, from a prepared position, resist LEA personnel. The acts that are committed in this situation will change the tactics used to dislodge the barricaded person. A barricaded person may be a sniper, a person with a hostage, a group of fanatics, or even a criminal caught in the act who takes the defensive from behind a counter in a department store. This manual gives methods by which persons who have barricaded themselves can be dislodged. By using techniques of room clearing, battle drill, building entry, stairwell clearing operations, individual combat practices, hostage rescue operations, anti-sniper drills, and background information (included and illustrated in this manual), a barricaded person can be dealt with.

Sequence of Actions: The following is normally applicable to a barricaded person situation by LEA personnel.

1) Officers arrive on the scene as a result of a call/complaint, dispatch, or personal observation. They will normally ascertain that the situation is that of a barricaded person.

2) As warranted, they will call for assistance, and make every effort possible to contain the situation. Units responding must be informed of the situation.

3) Units arriving at the scene will be directed to assemble at a safe area away from the barricaded site.

4) An Officer in Charge (OIC) will be dispatched to the scene. He will appraise the situation.

5) He will assign tasks as required to units at the scene (cordon of area, evacuation of civilians in area, establishing a command post, directing traffic, collecting information about the subject in question, etc.), and request any additional units and equipment to be dispatched to the scene.

6) Voice communication with the subject will be attempted. Passive efforts will be made to neutralize the situation. Members of the family may be brought in to talk to the subject if possible; clergymen, friends, psychologists, if able to communicate with the subject, should be considered.

If able to and the facilities exist, the barricaded person should be contacted by telephone (this lends a sense of normalcy).

7) During this time, blueprints of buildings are requested and studied, or someone familiar with the area is requested to draw a diagram of the building or area. Coordination is made to cut off power and other utilities if necessary. Special teams are briefed and moved into position. Special equipment is distributed or put into operation as required.

8) On the decision of the OIC, as a final resort, active measures are taken to dislodge the subject.

9) Minimal force required should be the rule of the day. However, officers of special teams or those assigned to neutralize the subject and situation must be prepared and equipped to use deadly force if absolutely necessary. The authorization to use deadly force must logically be a part of departmental policy, or the decision of the OIC on the scene and the leader of the unit assigned the mission of neutralizing the subject/situation.

NOTE: It is imperative that the first officers on the scene give adequate information to dispatch so that no responding unit arrives in the middle of a battlefield. As soon after the arrival of adequate backup units as possible, the area should be isolated (totally contained, innocents evacuated, and entire area cordoned). Every effort should be made to neutralize the situation passively. In some cases immediate active measures will be required to protect the lives of innocent persons in the immediate area. At these times passive measures, as required, will be dispensed with. If a command post is established, it must be far enough away from the scene of the incident to provide flexibility of movement for arriving units and a secure area in which to plan the operation.

PSYCHOLOGICAL CONSIDERATIONS IN HOSTAGE SITUATIONS

There are basically three personalities to deal with in hostage situations: The Criminal, the Sociopath (mentally unbalanced), and the Terrorist.

<u>The Criminal:</u> These individuals are caught in the act of committing a crime. They did not plan to take hostages. However, police arriving at the scene of the crime have more than likely blocked their avenue of escape. Realizing their situation as desperate, they will often take hostages to prevent their arrest, and have some bargaining power to perhaps make good an escape. In the beginning, a hostage situation of this type is quite possibly explosive. As time passes, the situation will tend to calm somewhat. It could be said that the longer the hostage spends with the offender in the contained position, the better. The more time the hostage spends with the felon in this manner, the better are the chances of the hostage's survival. It may be said that initially the offender has control of the situation. As time passes, the LEAs, through efforts to contain and isolate the situation and prepare the special teams and equipment available for possible action, gain control. The LEAs can make this shift calmly by keeping a low profile. Keep guns holstered unless necessary to have them out. Reduce the number of uniformed officers on the scene to only what is required. Keep special teams out of sight. Keep onlookers away. After the situation stabilizes the LEA should attempt to contact the offender and negotiate with him. Telephone is the best method of doing this. The negotiator should have the power to implement negotiation settlements with the offender to the limit of the jurisdictional policies of his department. Remember, the offender is surely afraid that he is going to die or be harmed. Only when things take on an appearance of normalcy can fruitful talks be conducted. When this happens the criminal will normally rationalize his plight and surrender his hostage.

NOTE: Offender must be sure that if he gives up he will not be killed. Normalcy must prevail. Police and special teams and equipment must keep a low profile. The criminal will be more likely to rationalize than any other personality that will be presented in this section.

The Sociopath: This type of individual is without a doubt the most dangerous personality to be confronted with in a hostage situation. Most of these type persons have a negative outlook towards society and mankind in general. It must be stressed that these type persons have no sense of right or wrong where they themselves are concerned. There is no contemplation of consequences. There is no reasoning as to the well being of anyone. These persons suffer from a totally inadequate personality. They have more than likely never been in a situation where they had total control. Therefore, the hostage situation is a new experience for them. They will normally have no idea how to handle it. This becomes a frustrating experience for a man who has difficulty controlling himself alone. It is apparent that having the added problems of controlling the hostage, attempting to control the situation, and maintaining some control of himself would be a tremendous strain on this man. For these reasons it is safe to say that his behavior will be predictably erratic. In some cases the hostage may represent a chance to prove that he is a man, or can accomplish something. On the other hand, this man may have feelings of self-destruction, and set up a hostage situation where he forces LEA personnel to take his life.

An example of the death wish is the skyjacker who makes impossible demands that he realized cannot be met. This is done to insure that the police will have to resolve the situation with deadly force; that is, the destruction of the sociopath. If LEAs are forced to terminate the situation with the use of deadly force, it is likely that a marked increase in similar incidents will happen in the future. Since these type situations are "good press" and sell newspapers, the resolving of the problem will receive wide coverage. This can result in what is defined as a Pandemic Situation, where other persons with suicidal tendencies see the hostage situation as the answer to their own desire to die.

Terrorists: Normally, these persons are politically, religiously, or socially oriented. There are certain traits that may assist the LEA in identifying them as terrorists and assist in indicating possible courses of action.

Hostage situations are normally well planned by these people. A target of some prominence is usually selected so that attention will be drawn to the situation. When this is accomplished they may state their cause to an audience of some size. They may also use this hostage as a bargaining tool. There are times when this group of personalities will secure unknown hostages. This act has the primary function of illustrating to the common man how vulnerable he is, even with the protection of police on the streets. Terrorists (normally operating in groups) are generally well armed, equipped and tactically prepared for the situation. They are likely to have deep convictions about their cause. The fact that they are a group also adds to their strength. They have been known to display a characteristic courage, and the ability to manipulate a situation to their advantage.

Since the terrorist/fanatic operates as a rule in groups, group dynamics may be a means to defeat them. If an aura of distrust can be created among them, it will weaken them tremendously. It may also be possible to create doubts about their cause, which will eventually cause collapse of the situation. News media should be given prepared statements by the OIC of the LEA at

the scene of a situation such as this. Very few terrorists/
fanatics will give their lives for a cause no one knows about.
It may be necessary to allow the subjects to talk to the media as
part of negotiations. The media should be made to understand
what the situation is and requested not to play the incident
up to grandiose levels.

A rule of thumb in a situation of this type is that if the subjects have more than one hostage (after the initial confrontation
with officers) and they should kill one, then it is more likely
than not that they will not hesitate to kill the remaining ones.

Hostage Negotiations: At the very onset of this period of instruction, it must be noted that there are at present numerous
operational practices and doctrines concerning this type of
mission.

It must be further stated that the policy of the city/munici-
pality, etc., will determine which approach its officers are to
adopt.

Hard-line Doctrine: The subject is engaged in conversation
(with bullhorn or from nearby, but from cover) while snipers
are moved into positions affording a one shot kill. If this
is indoors where a police marksman cannot observe the subject,
officers are moved to the building where they seek positions that
flank the gunman (FIGURE I). All of these actions may be carried
out while the subject is being talked to or after it has been
ascertained that talking will not work. Even if the subject
does not respond to talking, the noise of the bullhorn or someone's voice may distract him enough to enable SWAT members to
attain their positions with relative speed and safety. As soon as
marksmen are in position they should train their rifles on the

subject for a head shot. Remember, all else (talking, smoke, gas) has failed! Observe the subject. If at any time his weapon leaves the hostage, he can be dispatched. If body armor is available, a SWAT member may approach the subject, staying out of the line of fire of his marksman, and attempt to get the subject to draw down on him (FIGURE II). The main point of this technique is that once the subject and hostage are contained, they are not permitted to leave the area. The logic being that once out in the streets, dozens of potential hostages are available. During practical exercise in training, this should be covered extensively.

FIGURE I

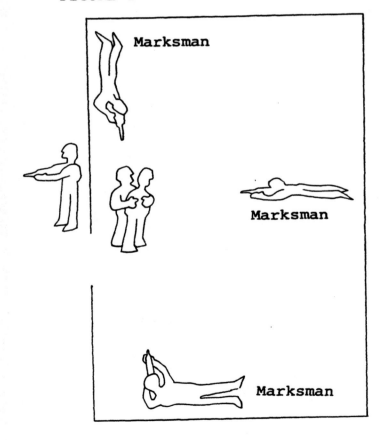

FIGURE II

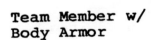

Team Member w/
Body Armor

Marksman

<u>Soft-line Procedure:</u> The SWAT operations in New York are essentially the same as in Los Angeles, but differ at the point that when everything short of exposing a SWAT member has been attempted and failed, the subject is permitted to move. The team will appease the subject to the most minimal degree that insures survival of the hostage. It must be noted that marksmen are continually prepared to take advantage of the head shot. Eventually, the subject will have to be dealt with. Perhaps he will have released the hostage. Perhaps he will have killed the hostage when this time comes, and have two or three more! An excellent point to bring out here is that members of New York's teams have been trained in basic and advanced psychology. Many times this is of tremendous value in determining the next move of the subject, and just how far the team can go without further jeopardizing the hostage.

HOSTAGE PROCEDURE

Street police will normally be the first to identify that the situation is in fact a hostage situation. It is extremely important that these first police to arrive at the scene are trained in what actions to take.

1) Contain the felon and his hostages with the minimum amount of personnel.
2) Establish an Inner Perimeter to further contain the subject.
3) Notify headquarters as to the situation.
4) Direct the placement of officers arriving at the scene.

   a) Inner Perimeter as required
   b) Assembly Area
   c) Outer Perimeter

   NOTE: These actions may be ordered by a senior commander if he arrives quickly. This is suggested.
5) Keep force (weapons, special teams, equipment) available in low profile.

OFFICERS RESPONDING TO A HOSTAGE SITUATION SHOULD COME WITHOUT
SIRENS OR LIGHTS.

Upon arrival of the senior commander, an assembly area will be
set up. This will be followed by the establishment of an outer
perimeter. This perimeter will keep innocents out of the area
of operations and act as a gathering/disposition point for personnel evacuated out of the area, by selected teams or officers.
It must be noted that the assembly area and the outer perimeter
must be located far enough away from the area of operations that
the felon cannot observe the actions that take place there.
All additional support personnel who arrive at the area of operations will be directed to report to the assembly area where a
command post will be operational.

The reason that all actions are taken to a low key is that the
hostage situation is definitely an explosive one. Initially
the felon has the upper hand. He is extremely excited and
worried for his safety. The appearance of numerous police personnel
or SWAT teams will do nothing more than further excite him,
possibly to the point where the hostage is killed. For this
reason weapons should be holstered at the scene as soon after
containing the felon as possible.

Once the containment is completed and if the hostage is still
all right, the balance of power begins shifting to the police
side. (FACT: The longer a hostage stays with a felon, the less
likely are the chances that the felon will kill him.) As the
situation stabilizes, those original street policemen will be
withdrawn from the inner perimeter and replaced with SWAT team
personnel. This must be done as inconspicuously as possible.
Once this is accomplished, the senior commander must decide
how he will handle the situation.

EXAMPLE OF DEPLOYED PERSONNEL

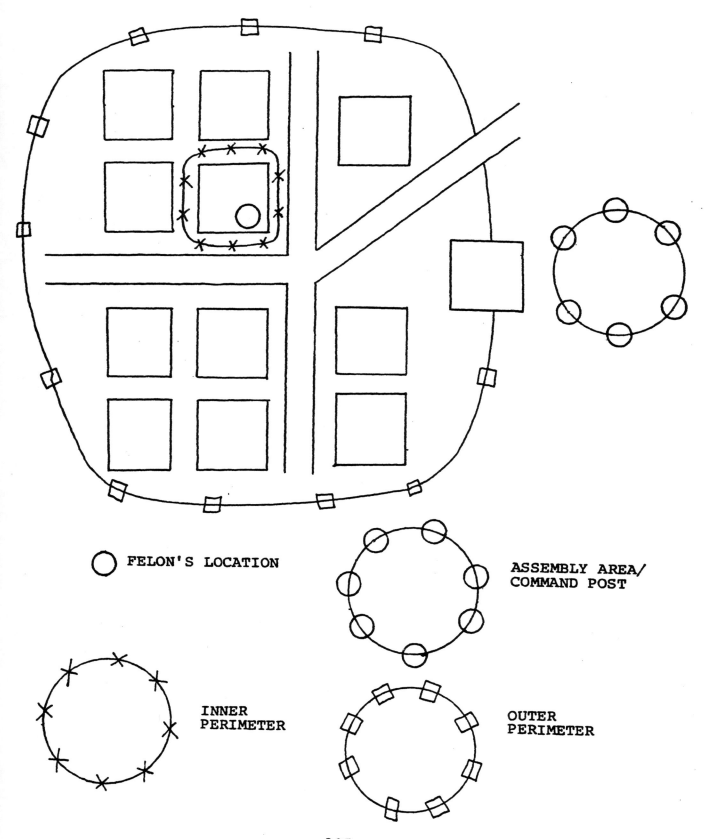

FELON'S LOCATION

ASSEMBLY AREA/
COMMAND POST

INNER
PERIMETER

OUTER
PERIMETER

If possible, negotiate. Contact the felon, preferably by phone.
You are buying time, to get floor plans, people who know the
felon, and to make plans. A competent man trained at negotiating
should talk to the felon and maintain communication. It must
be made clear to all of us that at no time will weapons be given
the felon, and at no time will police officers trade themselves
for the hostages. The negotiator should make the felon aware
that he is only a go between and that decisions will take time
from higher personnel. This will buy time for you and the hostage.
If the felon refuses to talk to a negotiator, try another person.
Try to keep the media out of the area as best as possible.
Their presence can give the felon renewed vigor. As time passes
a felon will get tired. He will also begin to fully understand
his plight and in most cases be able to rationalize. This is
the first step to resolving the situation.

During the time you have a negotiator talking to the felon, your
inner perimeter may close slightly to position themselves for
a one shot kill (should this be deemed necessary). Special
equipment should arrive at the assembly area during this time;
fire equipment, life squads, special tools and equipment. All
arrive without lights or siren. To minimize confusion, only
those required at the assembly area will be permitted to stay.
Other unnecessary policemen or agency personnel must leave and
resume their normal duties. Try to keep press personnel in
one location in the assembly area. Here a Senior Commander
can brief them as required.

Once all of the prior provisions have been accounted for, you
merely wait until you are ordered to assault the building or
the felon gives up. There may be some cases where the felon will
be allowed to move with a hostage in his control. In this situation, he is followed by trained personnel to any area where
he can again be contained. You may allow a felon to leave an

area due to there being many innocents in the area that could be hurt due to the felon's presence, i.e., a shopping center mall.)

MISCELLANEOUS FACTS

If a felon has a number of hostages and he kills one, it is almost a sure bet that he would kill those remaining. This action calls for immediate response with a single sniper kill shot or immediate building assault.

The best means in order of desirability to communicate with a felon holding a hostage are: Telephone (lends normalcy to the situation), face to face contact (have the negotiator wear CIVILIAN CLOTHES), bullhorn, radio, or television. If you must give the felon a police radio to communicate with you on, you must either use different frequency radios or another means of communications between those LEA people on the scene.

Negotiators must have authority to implement terms of negotiations within department jurisdictional scope.

The basic steps to resolving a hostage situation are:

CONTAIN   ISOLATE   APPREHEND

A reserve may be developed at the Command Post of personnel relieved from objective area.

Steps to follow:

    Establish inner perimeter.
    Establish outer perimeter of control.
    Decelerate the response of unneeded police personnel.
    Establish a Command Post.
    Evacuate civilians as necessary.
    Request negotiators, SWAT teams.
    Obtain all available information.
    Position special teams in best areas, replace inner perimeter.
      personnel with SWAT.
    Obtain the best tactical position possible.
    Negotiate.
    Prepare to react as required on order.

Isolated incidents: The felon has already isolated himself in one particular room of a large building or the top of a roof. In both cases police would have complete control over any avenue of exit that was available.

Three personality types; summary:

    The criminal: After initial confrontation, will usually rationalize.

    The terrorist/fanatic: Keep media away. Increases likelihood to kill. Very few will die for a cause with no publicity.

    The mentally unbalanced/sociopath: TOTALLY UNPREDICTABLE. HIGHLY DANGEROUS. Runs the gamut from being paranoid to schizophrenic--impulsive, approach with a rap as to what is best for him.

Stockholm Syndrome: Hostage sympathizes with felon. This is a phenomenon that all personnel should understand. For some reason, hostages who spend any length of time with a felon may begin to identify with that felon. They will sometimes indirectly or directly assist him. There are documented cases where hostages have refused to testify against the felon who held them, or did not take advantage of an opportunity to escape. Strange but true.

NIGHT VISION

Dark Adaptation: Allowing your eyes to become accustomed to low
levels of illumination. It takes thirty minutes for the rod
cells--those cells in your eye's retina that produce a chemical
substance called visual purple which helps activate the rod cells
and provide you with night vision--to become thoroughly adjusted.
If you are going into a darkened area from a lighted one and do
not have the time to let your eyes adjust, you may wear red tinted
goggles in the lighted area and remove them in the darkened area.
It will then take only five to ten minutes for your eyes to
adjust.

Once your eyes are adjusted to the dark, never look at a light
source. It takes only a second to lose your night vision. If
you must use a light, use one with a red lens. If you are exposed to light, close one eye and leave one open. This will pre-
serve the night vision in one eye.

Off Center Vision: The technique of keeping your attention on
an object without looking directly at it. When you look directly
at an object, the image is formed on the cone cells of the eye
which are non-functional during periods of low illumination.
By looking six to ten degrees off center of the object, the image
is formed on the rod cells, which allow you to see with the prod-
uction of visual purple. In effect you are looking out of the
side of your eye.

Scanning: Using off center vision to observe an object or area.
When you look off center of an object you will be able to see
that object for four to eight seconds before the visual purple
of the rod cells bleaches out in that particular area of the
eye. By moving your eyes every three to four seconds, you maintain constant visual purple without the bleaching effect.

If you wish to observe an object continuously, move your eyes
in short irregular movements all around the object at three to
four second intervals.

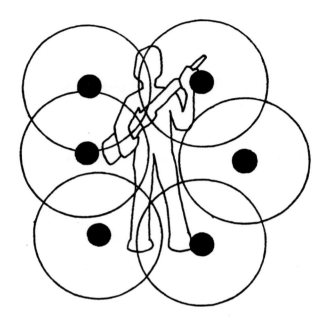

Black dots around the illustration of a man with a gun represent
points that you would look at. The larger circles around the
dots indicate what you would be able to see using off center
vision.

OPERATIONS IN A DARKENED AREA

Principles of movement by bounds with fire support still apply.

Operations are slowed to about one-third normal speed (with
exception to assault).

Listening halts are made frequently.

Distance between men is less than in daylight operations due
to control problems.

Artificial lighting devices are encouraged inside a building to
locate your suspect and rob him of his night vision. Outside
there may be instances where you would want to use illumination
to pinpoint your suspect.

When using light or firing your weapon in darkness, keep one eye closed. The flash of your weapon will affect your night vision. Keeping one eye closed when firing or using light will enable you to see after you have stopped firing.

Make maximum use of shadows (even in the dark).

Insure your equipment is silent.

Take the time to allow your eyes to adapt to the dark.

Control must be maintained. All men in your team must know the location of everyone else prior to firing.

Use simple plans that do not require the splitting up of your team. (This may be modified if artificial light is to be used.)

Be extremely careful of silhouetting yourself against light colored walls, cracks in doors, vents, fans, etc. Enough light will be there to provide your suspect a relatively clear target if his eyes have adapted to the dark.

Be alert for the exact location of your suspect's muzzle flash when he fires at you.

If he has a hostage, revert to normal hostage procedures. If you must assault him, use light. If he has no hostage, and you locate the muzzle flash of his weapon, direct maximum fire power in the direction of the flash.

Simulators are extremely effective at night.

Gas can be effective if all team personnel are equipped and prepared for its use.

Physical Exercise: Illustrate and demonstrate obtaining night vision, one on one in the dark, team movement, and artificial light use.

MISCELLANEOUS TIPS

If it should become necessary for your team to cross an alley or street which will expose you to your subject, throw a smoke grenade between your location and his and then have your entire team cross at once on the run.

In operations against what you know to be well equipped subjects, enter the building through a window, preferably top floor. Doors will more than likely be boobytrapped or very well covered.

Halt frequently for listening breaks in the building. Each man must take a good defensive position and then remain absolutely still for five to ten minutes. Quite often your subject will make some noise (cough, movement, etc.), which will assist you in locating him. Remember, in almost all cases he is going to be nervous also.

If you should be shot, lie absolutely still if you are at a point where you cannot reach cover and you are incapacitated. The subject will usually believe you are dead; thus so, you are reasonably safe.

When using smoke or gas outside, check wind speed and direction. If the wind is blowing toward you, throw the smoke well behind the subject. If it is to your back, throw it midway between the subject and your position. The same applies to gas.

When conducting large building (warehouse) operations, designate at least one man to observe up at all times.

Practice operations in your protective masks.

When in a building, touch nothing other than what is absolutely necessary. Boobytraps!

Always practice the habit of looking ten times then moving once.

When a man moves there should be at least one man covering him. Preferably two.

You must be able to use your weapon well in either hand.

In some large buildings the direction of a subject may be difficult to determine from the report of his weapon alone. Always observe for dust flying around the weapon and watch for a muzzle flash.

If you come upon an obstacle in a building (overturned tables in a hallway, debris), suspect that it is either boobytrapped or covered by the subject's fire.

Use smoke and gas whenever they will not put you at a disadvantage.

Use simulators as often as possible.

Utilize mirrors wherever and whenever possible.

Insure that if given an order you understand it completely! If you give an order insure that your men understand it completely.

BOOBYTRAPPING A DOOR

A very simple yet highly effective device for boobytrapping a door can be constructed using a common flashlight battery, an electrical blasting cap, an explosive compatible with the blasting cap, tape, insulated wire, and nails.

An explosive charge is taped to the wall near a door. A blasting cap is inserted. One wire from the blasting cap is attached to a battery which is also secured to the wall. From the negative side of the battery another wire is extended and stripped of insulation (at the very far end). A nail is attached to this bare end.

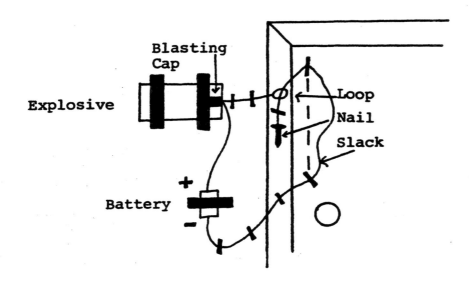

This wire is secured to the door frame and the door (leave two to three feet of slack between these points) with staples or nails. The other wire leading from the blasting cap is nailed to the frame of the door only. A loop is made at the very end of this piece of wire. The nail attached to the other wire (from the battery) is dropped through this loop. Only after the nail is through the loop and suspended away from the loop do you strip the loop of its insulation. When the door is opened the nail will be pulled into contact with the bare loop, completing the circuit and causing the explosive to activate.

A hand grenade is placed in a can of wet mud with the top of
the grenade and pin left exposed. The mud is allowed to dry
in the can around the grenade. When the mud is dried thoroughly,
mud and grenade (in one piece) are removed from can. Pin is
pulled, and mud with grenade inside is laid on a roof or in a
gutter/sewer. After a number of rainstorms, a sufficient amount
of mud washes off the grenade, allowing the arming lever to release,
activating the grenade. This may be weeks after the grenade is
emplaced.

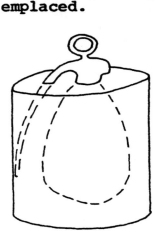  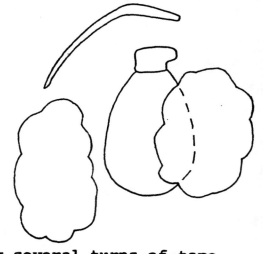

Grenade arming lever is taped down using several turns of tape.
Pin is pulled. The grenade may be left in a rubbish pile that is
to be burned. When tape is burned away from the arming lever the
grenade will activate. Again this may be days or weeks after
the grenade is emplaced. A grenade of this type may also be
placed in a tank of gas (usually a small grenade for gas tanks, on
the order of a military trip flare), where the gasoline will
dissolve the adhesive around the arming lever, allowing the
grenade to activate.

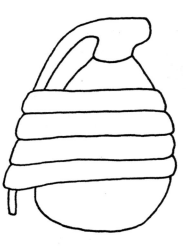

Arming lever
taped down,
pin removed.

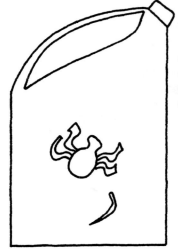

Gas dissolves
adhesive.
Grenade will
activate.

A cartridge/shell can be placed in a metal sleeve attached to a piece of wood with a nail in it (the nail acts as a firing pin) in such a manner than a small portion of the cartridge/shell extends above the sleeve. Putting pressure on the cartridge/shell forces the primer to strike the nail and fire the round in the direction the sleeve is oriented. This can be effective emplaced on stairs, behind drawers, doors, or randomly scattered in woods and fields.

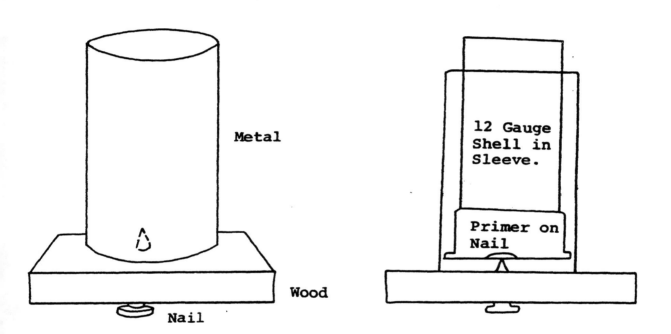

Metal

Wood

Nail

12 Gauge Shell in Sleeve.

Primer on Nail

Pressure of foot on shell will discharge the shell.

Another simple boobytrap is constructed by placing an obstacle
in front of a door that is likely to be opened during a search.
The obstacle is placed on top of a grenade so that its weight
depresses the arming lever. The safety pin is removed from
the grenade. When the obstacle is removed to gain access to the
door, the grenade activates. Most grenades will have a built
in time delay. However, there are those that will detonate
with no delay.

Use _extreme_ caution
anytime you are
forced to move an
obstacle. If poss-
ible, _always_ bypass
the obstacle.

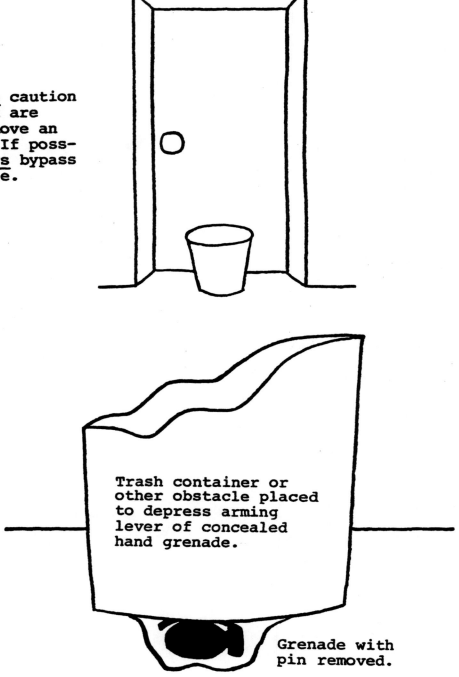

Trash container or
other obstacle placed
to depress arming
lever of concealed
hand grenade.

Grenade with
pin removed.

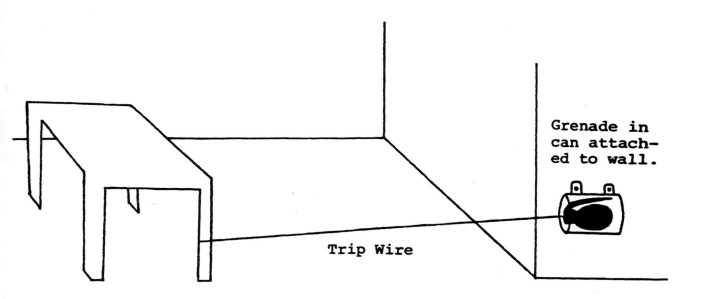

Grenade in can attached to wall.

Trip Wire

Another effective boobytrap that can be fabricated consists of a grenade, a #303 empty can and a trip wire. The can is attached to a fixed item, such as a wall or chair. A grenade is placed in the can. The grenade will fit perfectly in a #303 can. A trip wire is attached to the head of the grenade, not the safety pin. The trip wire is stretched over the terrain or area to be covered and tied off on a stationary object. At this time the safety pin is removed from the grenade while it is still in the can. The can is small enough that the arming lever will be depressed. Refer to the figure above.

When the trip wire is hit, the entire grenade will be pulled from the can, releasing the pressure that held the arming lever in place. The grenade will activate immediately and detonate in the time it takes for the delay fuze to burn. In some cases there will be no time delay--some grenades do not have time delay fuzes. Refer to the figure below.

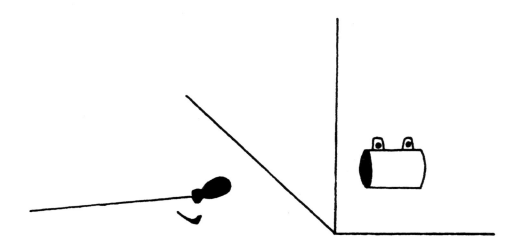

An extremely effective boobytrap may be fabricated out of a pressure type clothespin, a battery, a blasting cap, an explosive compatible to the blasting cap's ignition capability, and any insulative (current carrying capable) wire.

Secure a bare piece of wire on both the upper lip of the clothespin and the lower lip. This should be done in such a manner that when the clothespin is closed, the bare wires will make direct contact with one another. Insert a piece of wood or other non-conducting material between both lips of the clothespin to keep the two bare wires from making contact. Place clothespin on a peg, tree, or piece of furniture and secure in place. Use a nail, tape, or string. Stretch the trip wire out over the area you wish to cover. Again, check to make sure your wood peg is separating the two bare wires. Cut the wire as in the diagram near the explosive. Affix a blasting cap to the wire and place the cap into the explosive. Both ends where the cut was made must go into the blasting cap. Insure the wires running into the blasting cap are well secured. Make another cut in the wire near the power source as in the diagram below. Tape one piece of the wire to the positive side of the battery and the other piece to the negative side. When the trip wire is hit, the wood peg will fall out of the jaws of the clothespin, allowing both bare ends of the wire to touch. The circuit will be completed and the explosive will be detonated. This device can be command detonated by a person holding the trip wire at a great distance.

QUALIFIED EXPERTS ONLY should attempt to remove this device! IT IS UNSTABLE.

In practicing to set this device up, substitute a flashlight bulb for the explosive. If at any time during the setup the light comes on, you may say that the explosive would have been detonated.

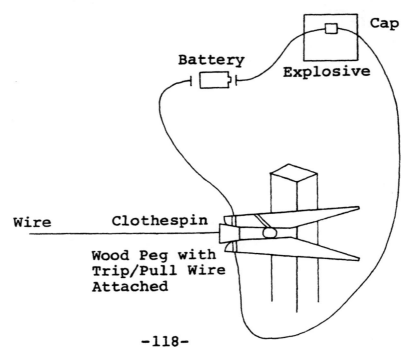

Cap

Battery

Explosive

Wire   Clothespin

Wood Peg with
Trip/Pull Wire
Attached

BOOBYTRAPPED LIGHT RECEPTACLE

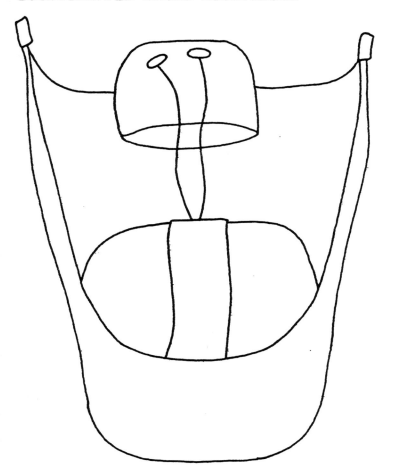

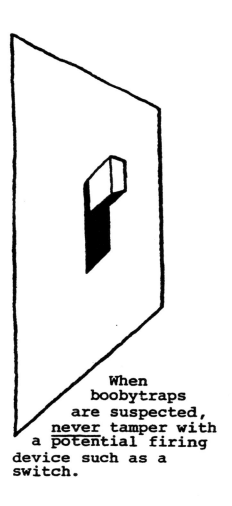

When boobytraps are suspected, never tamper with a potential firing device such as a switch.

A light bulb is removed from a light receptacle. The switch is off. From the ceiling an explosive is suspended (near the receptacle). An electric blasting cap is inserted into the charge and the wires from the cap are affixed to the inside of the receptacle, one to the contact and one to the side (inside). When the switch is turned on, the explosive will be activated.

By running the wires from the blasting cap and charge a long distance, into another room or another part of a building to attach them to a receptacle, the originator of this device can set it off much like a command detonated mine to injure or kill persons entering the other room. Suspect all wires that seem out of place. Be observant. If you are sure that this type of boobytrap exists, have the electric company shut off the power in the building.

Turn off
light.

Remove from
socket and
drill small
hole in upper
neck of bulb.

Fill with
gasoline or
black powder.
Plug hole with
cork or paper.

Screw bulb
back in
socket. Make
sure light is
out before
screwing in
bulb.

When light
is turned on
anyone in
room will be
killed or
injured.
Will also
start fire.

THE AUSTRALIAN CRAWL

In the conduct of normal SWAT operations, there may arise the
need to move from one building to another. Remembering that
entering a building from the top is the most favorable means,
it would in some cases be wasted energy to move out of the
building you were in and then attempt to climb up clear to
the top of the next one. By using a grappling hook and rappelling
rope, the Australian Crawl can be rigged in moments and will give
you the ability of getting to the next building without going
to ground level.

FIGURE I: The team in one building wants to reach the roof
of the next building about thirty feet away. The rappelling
rope is rigged onto the grappling hook, and the hook is thrown
across to the roof or through an open window (the hook will
break a closed window if thrown with enough force, therefore
the window could be closed). The hook is then set on the window
sill or ledge of the next building.

FIGURE II: The rope is pulled as taut as possible and secured
to a stationary fixture in/on the first building. Insure this
fixture is strongly emplaced, and insure that the rope is pulled
as taut as possible.

FIGURE THREE: While the remainder of the team covers the far
building, one team member hooks his D-ring (preferably locking)
onto the rope. (This man should have an automatic shotgun.)
He then lays out on the rope, hooking the instep (top of ankle)
of one foot over the rope. He allows his other leg to hang
free for balance. After practice the crawl can easily be negotiated with one hand. Once this man is on the rope he begins
an inchworm type movement by drawing his foot on the rope up
close to his buttocks, while at the same time reaching forward
with his hand/hands. Once this is done he pushes with his rear
foot and pulls with his hand/hands. He repeats this action
until he is across to the other building.

FIGURE IV: Upon reaching the other building, this man quickly
checks the room or roof out with his mirror, and then enters
and unhooks himself. He then provides security on the second
building while the rest of his team come across one at a time.

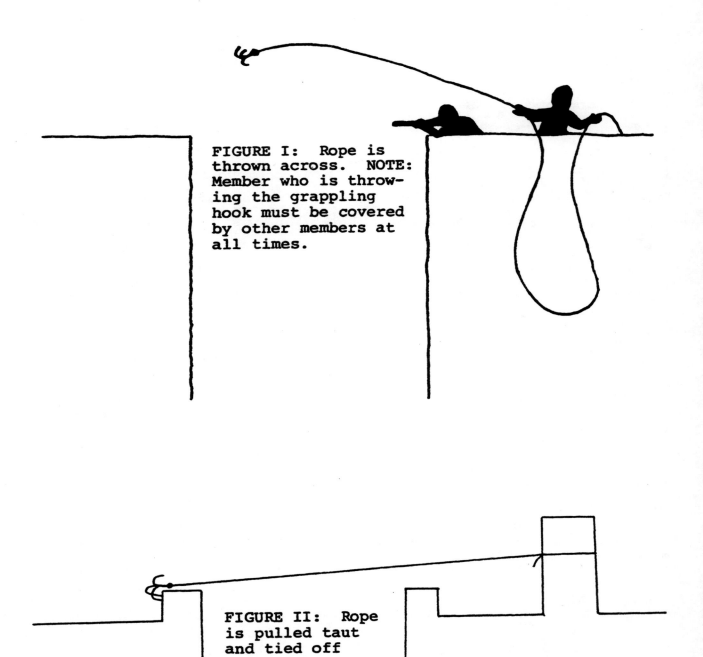

FIGURE I: Rope is thrown across. NOTE: Member who is throwing the grappling hook must be covered by other members at all times.

FIGURE II: Rope is pulled taut and tied off securely.

FIGURE III: Side view
of member on rope

NOTE: D-ring (preferably
locking) is attached to
man by swiss seat, and
locked onto rope.

Top view
of member
on rope

FIGURE IV: Man
reaches other side.
Observes and then
enters roof area.
NOTE: Other team
members cover his
movement.

FIGURE IV (cont.): First man across covers movement for next man across. When next man gets across, he will cover also.

If a man slips off the rope, he may get back up by locking one leg over the rope and swinging the other leg vigorously up and then down. On the down stroke he pulls his body up and again lays out on the top of the rope.

SWAT RAPPELLING PROCEDURES

In order to successfully complete your mission, it may become necessary to RAPPEL (also called ABSEIL) down the sides of buildings, cliffs, retaining walls, or similar vertical obstacles. Although rappelling will not be attempted under fire, there are several other difficulties to be considered. Safety, control, equipment weight, and ease of use are all important factors to be taken into account. The method selected for use by the SWAT teams, utilizing a "Swiss Seat" and Figure Eight Ring," provides the most acceptable combination of the previously mentioned factors. The equipment is light, relatively easy to use, and provides good control and safety while giving the added advantage of allowing one hand to be free to control weapons or other equipment.

EQUIPMENT

Figure Eight Ring: Issue: One per man.
                   Weight: 4.2 oz. (117 grams)
                   Strength: 9200 lbs.

Carabiner: Issue: One locking type or two non-locking type.
           Weight: 2 oz.
           Strength: 2200 lbs.

Nylon Webbing (seat and slings): Strength: 4000 lbs. (1"
                                           tubular webbing)

Kernmantle rope (also called "core and sheath"):
                                 Strength: 5000 lbs. (11mm)

Laid rope (also called "goldline"):
                                 Strength: 5025 lbs. (11mm) dry
                                           4500 lbs. (11mm) wet

ANCHORING

The method selected depends upon whether or not the rope will
be needed again for additional rappells during the mission.
If the team only needs to do a single rappel, the "figure-of-
eight" knot method can be used. The doubled rope method can also
be used for a single rappel; it must be used when the rope is
needed for additional rappelling during the mission. Several
webbing slings and carabiners will also be needed in either case.

Slings are webbing loops tied together with a doubled overhand
knot (see B-E below). In anchoring, the sling is tied first;
then passed around the anchor. Several slings can be tied
together if one is not sufficient to pass around the anchor.
The looped ends of the sling are then joined together and to
the rope with one locking carabiner or two non-locking carabiners. NEVER join rope directly with a sling. The heat caused
by the rope passing directly over the webbing will weaken or
break the sling.

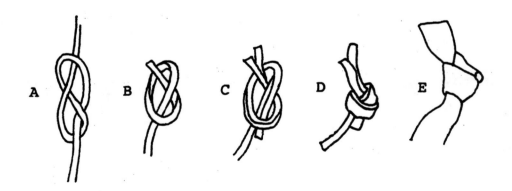

Figure-of-Eight Knot (A).
Doubled Overhand Knot (B-E), used for BOTH slings and "Swiss
seats."

If only one rappel is to be made, a Figure-of-Eight knot can
be tied in the end of the rope. The carabiner is then locked
into the loop of the knot. Be certain to tie the knot tightly
and leave a six to twelve-inch section of rope on the side of
the knot.

If the rope must be used again, the midpoint of the rope is locked
into the carabiner. The rope can then later be pulled through
from below.

In the event that no single solid anchor can be found, several
weaker anchors can be joined together by slings. In this case
as in all others, the anchors should be tested prior to the
rappel to be certain they will support a man's weight.

FIGURE EIGHT RING (FIGURES I,II,III)

Bearing in mind FIGURE I-A, take a bight (pronounced "bite")
in the rope and pass it through the upper oval ring. Pull it
down as shown in FIGURE I-B and pull the ring through the en-
larged bight. Attach the carabiners to the Swiss seat and
the lower (smaller) ring. Grasp the rope with control hand
and rappel. This same basic configuration is used if you intend
to use the ring for belay, load lowering, etc. FIGURE II-A
shows the normal configuration for applying friction on rappel.
FIGURE II-B shows the small diameter double rope lock configuration or 11mm single lock, and II-C shows the configuration
for locking if you are using a double 8 or 9mm or in some cases
for single 10.5 or 11mm. FIGURE III-A shows the use of a single
9mm, FIGURE III-B shows double 9mm in use, FIGURE III-C shows
single 11mm in use, and FIGURE III-D shows double 7/16 laid
rope.

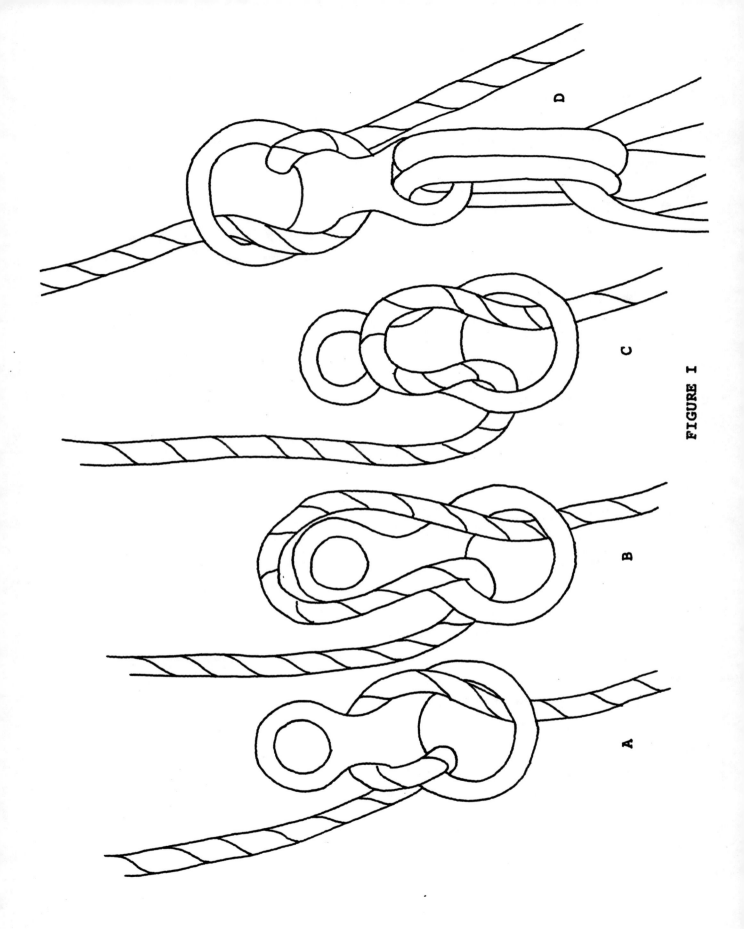

FIGURE I

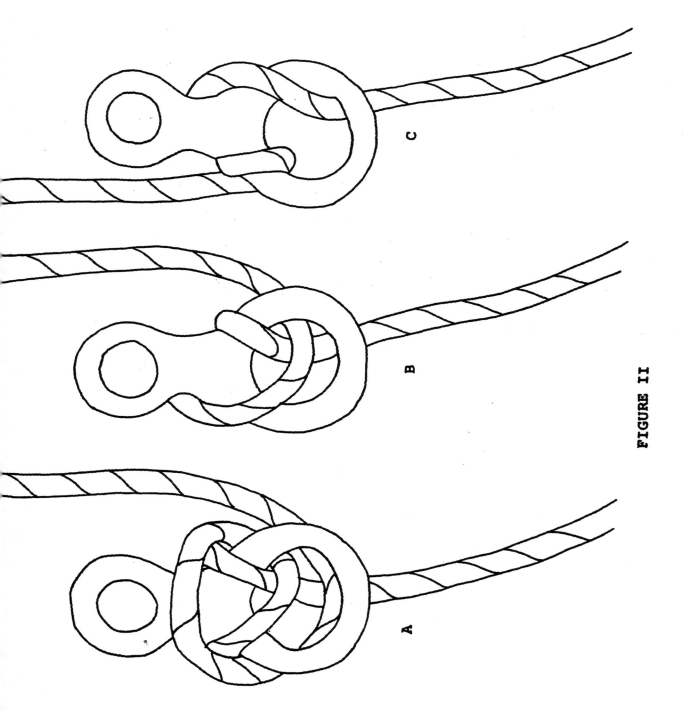

FIGURE II

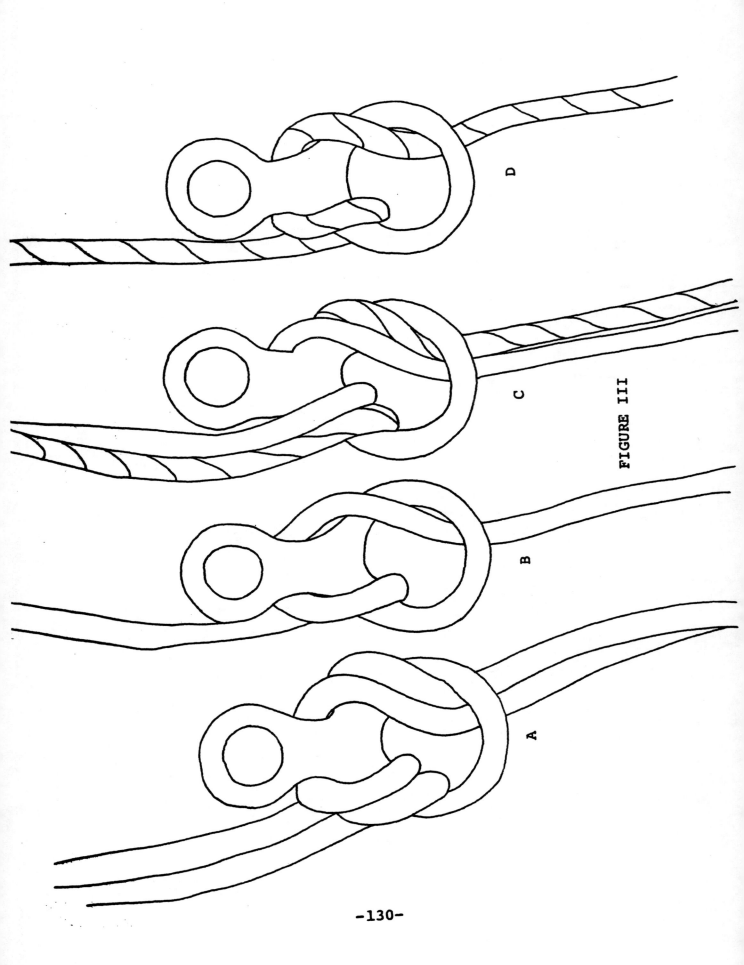

FIGURE III

SWISS SEAT

To make the Swiss seat, nylon webbing is tied in a loop with
a doubled overhand knot. Pass the open loop over your buttocks
and then pull another loop up through your crotch. Pass a
carabiner through the three loops from left to right. The
carabiner can then be attached to the small end of the figure
eight ring. The seat should fit tightly.

RAPPELLING

After the seat is attached to the ring on the rope, step over
the rope so that it runs through your crotch. Grasp the rope
with your right hand below your buttocks; this will be the
controlling hand. Your other hand is free and NOT to be used.
Lower yourself until you make a forty-five degree angle with
the wall; then begin walking down the wall playing out the rope
as you go.

GENERAL NOTES

NEVER step on rope or expose it to gritty surfaces, as this
cuts some of the fibers and weakens the rope. In the event
that a fall or other severe strain is placed on the rope,
it should be discarded.

If a locking carabiner is not available, use two non-locking
ones with gates facing in opposite directions.

PITON USE

As a general rule you should drive a piton in until the eye of the piton is flush with the anchor surface.

USE ANGLE PITONS IN CONCRETE BLOCKS AND VERTICAL CRACKS.

USE OFFSET PITONS IN WOOD AND HORIZONTAL CRACKS.

USE BOLTS IN REINFORCED CONCRETE OR SOLID ROCK.

ANGLE PITONS
FOR BLOCK

OFFSET PITONS
FOR WOOD

PITON HAMMER

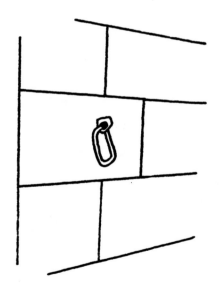

ANGLE PITON IN
BLOCK WALL

OFFSET PITONS IN
WOOD, TIED TOGETHER
FOR MAXIMUM STRENGTH

Drive pitons in floors, walls or ceilings **IF** they are:

Wood

Concrete Block

Brick

Place a sturdy object (desk, filing cabinet, water cooler, etc.) too large to fit through the opening in front of it and wrap it with daisy chains.

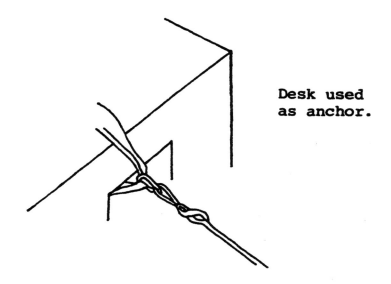

Desk used as anchor.

THE ROOF

Many objects may be found on most roofs to use as anchors. These include:

Chimneys

Vents

Electrical Distribution Posts

Air Conditioning Equipment

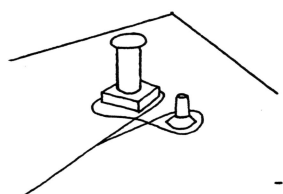

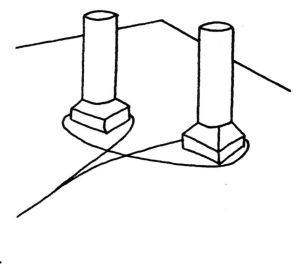

GLOSSARY

RUNNER OR SLING--An endless loop made of webbing which is six feet in circumference.

DAISY CHAIN--A series of runners.

CARABINER, BINER, OR KRAB--A snap link.

PITON--A nail of varying design made of iron or chrome moly with an eye in the end instead of a head.

ALWAYS   Set your knots.

Pad sharp edges.

Use multiple anchors.

NEVER   Allow a rope to work against a sharp edge.

Rig the rope through the sling. Always use a carabiner to join them.

Use a single anchor!

CHECKLIST   TEST ALL ANCHORS!

TEST ALL KNOTS!

ARE YOUR ANCHORS SECURE?

ARE YOUR KNOTS SET?

ARE ALL SHARP EDGES PADDED?

Annex A: Physical Fitness Proficiency Test

1 Mile Run: Passing this test must be accomplished with full equipment that would be carried into a combat situation, within 10 minutes. Pass/Fail grade only.

40 yd Low Crawl: This must be completed in less than 28 seconds. Must include wearing of combat boots and web gear. If weapon is carried maximum time is extended to 30 seconds.

Sit-Ups: 50 in two minutes. Bent leg style.

Push-Ups: 30 in one minute.

Rope Climb: Climb 20 feet vertically (free climb) within 30 seconds.

Must be able to fully complete 2 minutes of grass drill with all equipment.

The above exercises/tasks lend themselves to fully conditioning the members of a team and are geared toward physical activities that would be associated with an actual mission.